C0-ANC-902

EXECUTIVE
Mike Mifsud, Alan Doan, Jenny Doan,
Sarah Galbraith, David Mifsud

MANAGING EDITOR
Natalie Earnheart

CREATIVE DIRECTOR
Christine Ricks

PHOTOGRAPHY TEAM
Mike Brunner, Lauren Dorton, Jennifer Dowling,
Dustin Weant

PATTERN TEAM
Edie McGinnis, Denise Lane, Jessica Toye,
Tyler MacBeth

PROJECT DESIGN TEAM
Jenny Doan, Natalie Earnheart

EDITORS & COPYWRITERS
Camille Maddox, Nichole Spravzoff, David Litherland

SEWIST TEAM
Jenny Doan, Natalie Earnheart, Carol Henderson,
Janice Richardson

QUILTING & BINDING DEPARTMENT
Becky Bowen, Glenda Rorabough, Nikki LaPiana,
Amy Turpin, Debbie Elder, Holly Clevenger, Kristen
Cash, Todd Harman, Jessica Paup, Jan Meek, Linda
Frump, Franny Fleming, Rachael Joyce, Selena Smiley,
Nora Clutter, Lyndia Lovell, Jackie Jones, Roxanna
Hinkle, Deloris Burnett, Bernice Kelley, Darlene Smith,
Janet Yamamoto

LOCATION CREDIT
Mari's House B&B Hamilton, MO
Duncan's Berry Farm, Smithville, MO
Hamilton R2 in C/O Troy Ford, Hamilton, MO
Elizabeth Plotner, Davies County Library, Gallatin MO

PRINTING COORDINATORS
Rob Stoebener, Seann Dwyer

PRINTING SERVICES
Walsworth Print Group
803 South Missouri
Marceline, MO 64658

CONTACT US
Missouri Star Quilt Company
114 N Davis
Hamilton, MO 64644
888-571-1122
info@missouriquiltco.com

content

Oops! Sometimes we make mistakes.
To find corrections to every issue of Block
go to: www.msqc.co/corrections

hello
from MSQC

Long and lazy, summer days almost feel like a dream. I can't think of a better wake-up call than when I arise in the morning to the hum of a lawnmower and the smell of freshly cut grass. The air is already warm and I'm tempted to have ice cream for breakfast. Off in the distance, I can hear the familiar *tic-tic-tic* of a sprinkler watering the garden. I want to savor every moment, soaking up the sunshine, and drawing every bit of enjoyment out of those fleeting days. It may not be a time when I feel like snuggling up under a quilt, but it's definitely an inspiring time.

With bright colors and perhaps a bit more free time than usual, I see summer as a time for inspiration and planning. Fall is when I want to settle in and really get sewing in anticipation for winter, but in the summer I want to snap up all the gorgeous fabrics I see! Bold florals and pretty prints take over my mind and I start seeing quilts form in my imagination. I see shapes everywhere I go, hidden in between fence slats and cracks in the pavement, shimmering in the tiles of a swimming pool.

The vivid colors of summer, in contrast to the pastels of spring, fill me with energy! I almost want to taste a delicious shade of fuschia when I see it. Colors stand out to me everywhere I go, in the stripes of a beach towel, in fresh flowers, and sweet icy treats. I hope your summer is filled with plenty of fun and a good dose of inspiration.

Jenny

JENNY DOAN
MISSOURI STAR QUILT CO.

For the tutorial and everything you need to make this quilt visit:
www.msqc.co/blocksummer19

vintage
blossom

Summer sneaks in kind of slowly. It starts with brisk mornings that transform into sweaty afternoons. The sun wakes up earlier each day, and goes to bed later and later. The grandkids finish school for the year and we fall into a routine of play, play, play!

It is during these first few days of warm weather that my dear friend, RuthAnn, starts her garden. She plants seeds in neat, straight rows and waters them with care. Every evening after dinner, she heads outside to weed and tend her garden. As delicate sprouts start to pop through the soil, she feels a little impatient, dreaming of juicy tomatoes and sweet corn on the cob.

Summer wears on, and things start to get hot. Too hot. The sun beats down mercilessly on her young garden, but, somehow, those hardy plants flourish in the midsummer heat. She starts to notice tiny green tomatoes here and there. Big, orange blooms pop open on her squash plants. Corn stalks race toward the sky. She weeds and waters day by day, still dreaming of the harvest.

The berries come first. Right around the Fourth of July, her raspberry bushes come alive with big, juicy berries. When she wakes up in the morning, she heads outside to pick a handful to eat with her eggs and toast.

At lunchtime, the grandkids come over for a swim. Two little sweethearts with floaties on their arms climb into the water, circle the pool twice, then climb back out and race toward the raspberry bushes. Then it's back into the swimming pool and over to the raspberries again. Repeat, repeat, repeat. Their chubby cheeks are stained with raspberry juice, their hands are sticky, and they're just about the happiest kids you've ever seen.

Weeks pass and the berries are gone, but they are quickly replaced with a rainbow of fresh produce. RuthAnn feasts on tomatoes still warm from the summer sun and corn that literally bursts with flavor in her mouth. She fries up zucchini with yellow squash and onions. She eats every meal fresh from the garden, a rich reward for a summer of waiting.

As the harvest increases, she shares her abundance with neighbors and relatives. She preserves pickles and salsa and sliced peaches in glass jars. Little by little, the garden slows down. The sun shines more gently. The days grow shorter. Once again, there is a chill in the morning air. Summer slips away, just as subtly as it came, leaving behind nothing but memories and those neat rows of newly-filled Mason jars on the cellar shelves.

materials

QUILT SIZE
70" x 84"

BLOCK SIZE
12" finished

QUILT TOP
4 packages 5" print squares
1 roll 2½" background strips
   -includes inner border

OUTER BORDER
1½ yards

BINDING
¾ yard

BACKING
5¼ yards - vertical seam(s)

OTHER
Missouri Star Small Half-Hexagon Template

SAMPLE QUILT
Red and Blue...and Roses Too! by Faye Burgos for Marcus Fabrics

1 cut

Set aside (25) 5" print squares for another project.

Select (3) matching 5" print squares. Cut each square in half vertically and horizontally to make 2½" squares. Each 5" square will yield 4 squares and a **total of 12** squares are needed. Set aside to use when making horizontal sashing strips.

Fold the remaining (140) 5" squares in half. Place the template on the folded square and cut around the shape. Each folded square will yield 2 half-hexagons and a **total of 280** are needed. Keep all matching prints together.

1A

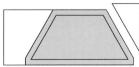

2A

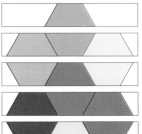

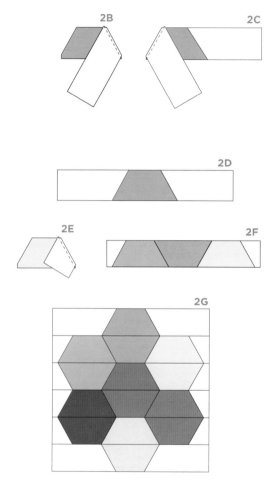

2B 2C

2D

2E 2F

2G

From (11) 2½″ background strips, cut 10 strips into 2½″ x 12½″ rectangles. Subcut (1) 2½″ x 12½″ rectangle from the remaining strip. You will have a **total of 31** rectangles. Set them aside to use for sashing.

From (9) 2½″ background strips, use the half-hexagon template to subcut each strip into half-hexagons.
Note: you will have to flip the template 180° with each cut. Each strip will yield

9 half-hexagons and a **total of 80** are needed. Cut each half-hexagon in half to make 2 quarter-hexagons for a **total of 160.**

From each of (13) 2½″ background strips, cut (6) 2½″ x 6″ rectangles. Pick up the remainder of the 2½″ strip from which you cut the 2½″ x 12½″ rectangle. Cut (2) 2½″ x 6″ rectangles and add them to the stack you have already cut. You should have a **total of 80** rectangles.

Set aside the remaining 7 background strips for the inner border.

Pair (2) 2½″ x 6″ rectangles with wrong sides facing. Using the half-hexagon template, align the squared-off portion with 1 end of the strip and cut the angle. **Note:** by layering the rectangles, you will have mirror image angles. That will give you angled rectangles for both sides of each row where needed. **1A**

2 block construction

Pick up 7 pairs of print half-hexagons, 8 background quarter-hexagons, 2 sets of angled 2½″ x 6″ rectangles.

Lay out the block in rows as shown in the diagram. Be sure the longest edges of the matching print half-hexagons line up from row to row so a complete hexagon is formed. **2A**

Begin and end rows 1 and 6 with angled rectangles. Align the slanted edge of the angled rectangle to the half-hexagon with right sides facing. Offset the 2 pieces at the ¼″ seam line and sew the pieces together. Repeat for the other side of the half-hexagon. **2B 2C 2D**

Rows 2 through 5 are made up of 3 half-hexagons and begin and end with a quarter-hexagon. Align the slanted edge of a quarter-hexagon with the slanted edge of a half-hexagon with right sides facing. Offset the 2 pieces at the ¼″ seam line and sew the pieces together. Continue in this manner until you have sewn the pieces in each row together. Press the seams of the odd rows in 1 direction and the seams of the even rows in the opposite direction to make the seams nest. **2E 2F**

Sew the rows together. Square up the block to 12½″. **2G**
Make 20 blocks.

Block Size: 12″ finished

3 arrange and sew

Pick up the 2½″ x 12½″ background rectangles you set aside earlier. Lay out the blocks in **5 rows of 4** and add a 2½″ x 12½″ sashing rectangle between each block vertically. Sew each row together. Press all seam allowances toward the sashing rectangles.

11

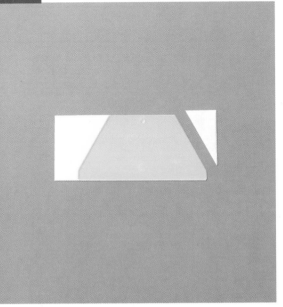

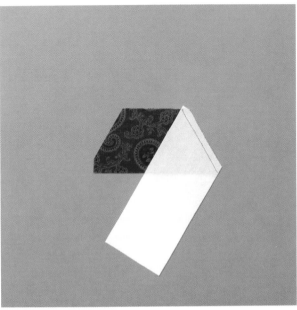

1 Pair (2) 2½" x 6" background rectangles with wrong sides facing. Align the half-hexagon template with 1 end of the rectangles and cut the angle.

2 Align the slanted edge of an angled rectangle to the print half-hexagon with right sides facing. Offset the 2 pieces at the ¼" seam line and sew the pieces together.

3 Add an angled rectangle to the other side of the half-hexagon to complete the row.

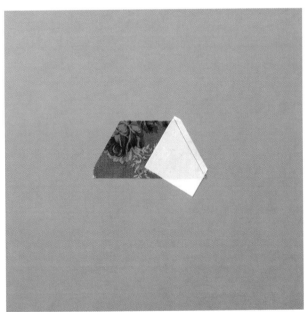

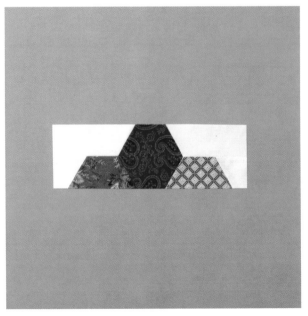

4 Begin and end rows 2 through 5 by sewing a quarter-hexagon to a print half-hexagon.

5 As you lay out the rows, make sure the longest edges of matching print half-hexagons line up from row to row so a complete hexagon is formed.

Make horizontal sashing strips. Begin the strip by sewing a 2½" x 12½" background rectangle to a 2½" print square. Continue alternating the rectangles and squares until the strip is made up of 4 rectangles and 3 squares. Press all seam allowances toward the sashing rectangles. **Make 4** horizontal sashing strips. **3A**

Sew the rows together adding a horizontal sashing strip between each row to complete the center of the quilt.

4 inner border

Pick up the (7) 2½" background strips you set aside earlier. Sew the strips together end-to-end to make 1 long strip. Trim the borders from this strip.

Refer to Borders (pg. 102) in the Construction Basics to measure and cut the inner borders. The strips are approximately 68½" for the sides and approximately 58½" for the top and bottom.

5 outer border

Cut (8) 6½" strips across the width of the fabric. Sew the strips together end-to-end to make 1 long strip. Trim the borders from this strip.

Refer to Borders (pg. 102) in the Construction Basics to measure and cut the outer borders. The strips are approximately 72½" for the sides and approximately 70½" for the top and bottom.

6 quilt and bind

Layer the quilt with batting and backing and quilt. After the quilting is complete, square up the quilt and trim away all excess batting and backing. Add binding to complete the quilt. See Construction Basics (pg. 102) for binding instructions.

For the tutorial and everything you need to make this quilt visit:

www.msqc.co/blocksummer19

courtyard
path

Nine-year-old Ben Sampson had been missing his dad for a long time. As a member of the United States Army, Dad had been deployed before, but this time Ben was old enough to really feel his absence in the simple goings-on of day-to-day life.

Dad left at the end of September. He missed Halloween. Ben's mom tried to help with the pumpkin carving, but it just wasn't the same. He missed Thanksgiving and Christmas. He missed Ben's birthday in February. But for some reason, those weren't the days that hurt the most.

Ben missed his dad when he woke up to winter's first big storm. He tried to build a snowman by himself, but he couldn't get the snow to roll right.

He missed his dad when their favorite college basketball team made it to the championship game.

Worst of all, Ben missed his dad when they passed out Pinewood Derby kits at Cub Scouts. How would he shape that block of wood into a winning race car all by himself?

That's when Carl showed up. Carl was a retired army man himself. He lived next door and kept busy puttering in his garage. He was a quiet sort of fellow, but when word spread that Ben was worried about his woodworking project, Carl brushed the sawdust off his overalls and marched across the lawn to offer his help. The two of them planned and created an amazing cherry-red '57 Thunderbird derby car. And that was just the beginning.

Carl and Ben became inseparable. Carl taught Ben how to tie flies for his fishing rod. Ben taught Carl how to get to the secret level on his favorite racing video game. Carl brought over homegrown tomatoes and his wife's freshly baked bread. Ben helped paint Carl's new shed. It was an unlikely friendship, but they filled a void in each other's lives, and it was sweet to see.

When Father's Day rolled around, Ben started to get that familiar feeling in the pit of his stomach. His dad had been deployed for nine months, and missing someone that long

was a hard chore for a young boy. Luckily, his mom had a great idea. She said, "Why don't you do something special for Carl for Father's Day? His own grandchildren live so far away. I'm sure it would mean a lot."

When Carl awoke on Father's Day morning, he looked out the window to see a freshly mown lawn. The weeds had been cleared from his vegetable garden, and the walkway was swept clean.

The doorbell rang. On the porch was a plate of chocolate donuts with a note that read, "Happy Father's Day! Thanks for being my almost-grandpa!" Out of the corner of his eye, Carl spied Ben peeking out from behind his maple tree.

It took a bit of effort, but Ben's mom's plan had worked! The heartache of that day melted away, leaving plenty of room for a shared plate of chocolate donuts.

materials

QUILT SIZE
79" x 95"

BLOCK SIZE
8" finished

QUILT TOP
1 package 10" print squares
1 package 10" background squares

INNER BORDER
¾ yard

OUTER BORDER
1¾ yards

BINDING
¾ yard

BACKING
8½ yards - vertical seam(s) - or 3 yards of 108" wide

OTHER SUPPLIES
Missouri Star Drunkard's Path Small Circle Template Set

SAMPLE QUILT
Misty by Chong-a Hwang for Timeless Treasures

1 layer and cut

Layer a background square with a print square. Align the 8½" mark of template A on 1 corner of the layered squares. Cut around the 2 sides of the template and the curve. Place template B on the remaining corner of the layered squares. Align the 2 edges with the corner of the squares. Cut along the curve. Repeat for the remaining squares. You will have a **total of 40** each of the A and B pieces cut from prints and a **total of 40** each of the A and B pieces cut from the background. **1A**

2 block construction

Pair all background A pieces with print B pieces and all print A pieces with background B pieces.

Pick up an A/B set. Fold each piece in half on the diagonal and finger press to mark the midway point of each curved edge. Place the A piece on top of the B piece with right sides facing and finger pressed centers aligned. Pin at the center point and at both ends of the seam allowance. **2A**

Stitch the 2 pieces together along the curve. Use your fingers to ease in the

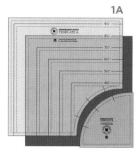

1A

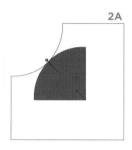

2A

2B

fullness around the curve and avoid stretching the fabric as you sew. Press the seam allowance towards the A piece.

Make a **total of 80** blocks. **2B**

Block Size: 8″ finished

3 arrange and sew

Refer to the diagram on page 21 and lay out the blocks in rows, paying particular attention to how each block is oriented. Each row is made up of **8 blocks** and **10 rows** are needed. After the blocks have been sewn into rows, press the seam allowances of the odd-numbered rows toward the right and the even-numbered rows toward the left to make the seams nest.

Sew the rows together to complete the center of the quilt.

4 inner border

Cut (8) 2½″ strips across the width of the fabric. Sew the strips together end-to-end to make 1 long strip. Trim the borders from this strip.

Refer to Borders (pg. 102) in the Construction Basics to measure and cut the inner borders. The strips are approximately 80½″ for the sides and approximately 68½″ for the top and bottom.

5 outer border

Cut (9) 6″ strips across the width of the fabric. Sew the strips together end-to-end to make 1 long strip. Trim the borders from this strip.

Refer to Borders (pg. 102) in the Construction Basics to measure and cut the outer borders. The strips are approximately 84½″ for the sides and approximately 79½″ for the top and bottom.

6 quilt and bind

Layer the quilt with batting and backing and quilt. After the quilting is complete, square up the quilt and trim away all excess batting and backing. Add binding to complete the quilt. See Construction Basics (pg. 102) for binding instructions.

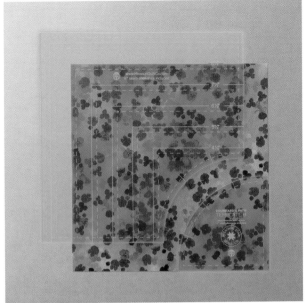

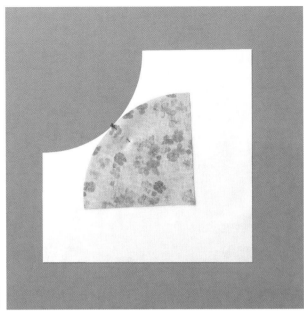

1 Layer a 10" background square with a 10" print square with right sides facing. Align the 8½" mark of template A on 1 corner of the layered squares. Cut around the template. Place template B on the remaining corner of the layered squares. Cut around the curve.

2 Pick up an A/B set. Fold each piece in half on the diagonal and finger press to mark the midway point of each curved edge. Place the A piece on top of the B piece with right sides facing and finger pressed centers aligned. Pin at the center point and at both ends of the seam allowance.

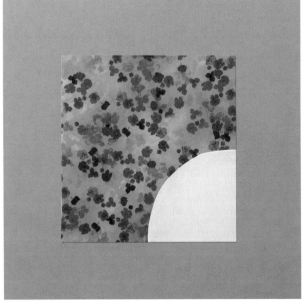

3 Stitch the 2 pieces together along the curve. Use your fingers to ease in the fullness around the curve, being careful to avoid stretching the fabric as you sew.

4 Make a total of 80 blocks, 40 using background A pieces and 40 using print A pieces.

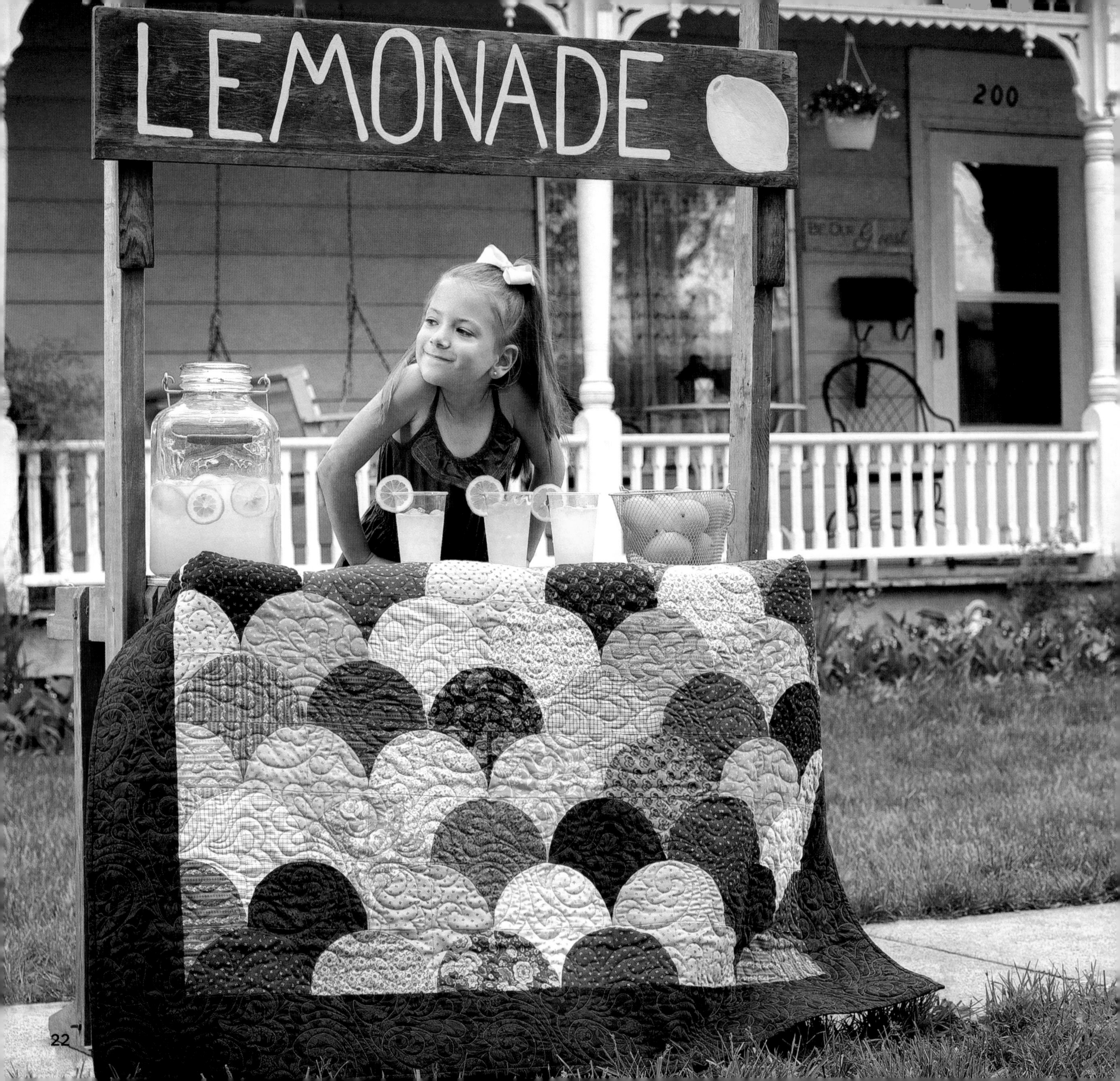
LEMONADE
200

For the tutorial and everything you need to make this quilt visit:
www.msqc.co/blocksummer19

easy clamshell

When Candice Johnson was ten years old, she and her sisters cooked up a genius summer plan: They would open up a lemonade stand on their front lawn, earn enough cash to buy passes to the local wave pool, and spend the rest of the summer splashing, floating, and giggling at handsome lifeguards.

The trio scurried to gather supplies while their mother was out running errands. A folding card table was pulled out of the back of the garage, wiped down, and covered with a quilt. Everyone agreed that Candice had the best handwriting, so she got to work on the sign while Kelly and Michelle stirred up a pitcher of lemonade.

Candice carefully formed the most beautiful fancy lettering she could manage: "Lemonade: 25¢." Paper cups were lined up in neat rows, ice cubes bobbed in the pitcher, and an empty mason jar stood, ready to be filled with the day's plunder.

Unfortunately, the Johnson family lived on a dead end street in the corner of a sleepy little town. On a busy day, a car or two wandered down the lane just to make a u-turn and continue their journey elsewhere. Most days, however, Blackberry Circle was quiet.

Nevertheless, the girls set up lawn chairs and awaited their customers.

Minutes passed. Nothing. An hour passed. Still nothing. Finally, they heard the familiar putter of the mail truck heading toward their street. "The mailman's coming! Quick, grab the sign! He's sure to stop for a lemonade!" And he did!

Candice carefully filled a little paper cup all the way to the brim. Mr. Gregory gulped it down in one big swallow and bought a second serving to go. Candice squeezed those two shiny quarters in her hand. "We're going to be rich!"

Her excitement, however, did not last. The rest of the day was dismally uneventful. The girls sold one cup of lemonade to old Mrs. Lewis who was taking her cranky dachshund for a walk, and another cup to Mom when she returned home from her errands.

When all was said and done, the Johnson sisters had earned a total of $1—a full $59 short of their goal. But did they give up? Heavens, no! The very next weekend, with the help of their mother, they moved their lemonade stand to a brand new location: the finish line of the Founder's Day parade. After walking the entire parade route in 90-degree weather, folks were clamoring to buy a cup of lemonade. Some sweaty customers bought three, four, or five cups!

That night, Candice poured the quarters out on her bed. "We've got 65 dollars!" she squealed. And so, you guessed it! They lived happily ever after—or at least all summer long—in the delightfully cool waters of the Lakeland Community Wave Pool.

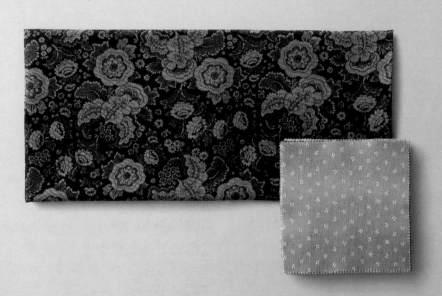

materials

QUILT SIZE
59" x 67"

BLOCK SIZE
4" finished

QUILT TOP
4 matching packages 5" print squares

BORDER
1¼ yards

BINDING
¾ yard

BACKING
3¾ yards - horizontal seam(s)

OTHER
Missouri Star Drunkard's Path Small
  Circle Template Set

SAMPLE QUILT
Regency Sussex by Christopher
Wilson-Tate for Moda Fabrics

1 cut

Select 2 matching 5" print squares. Place
Template B on the lower right corner of 1 of
the squares and cut around the curve. After
you have cut the curve, align the 4½" mark
on Template A on the upper left corner of
the square and cut the inner curve. Repeat
for the matching square you selected. Keep
all matching prints together! **1A 1B**

Repeat the cutting instructions for all the
remaining 5" squares. Be sure to keep all
matching prints together. You will have a
total of 168 A pieces and **168** B pieces.

1A

1B

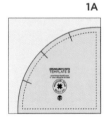

2 lay out the quilt

Each clamshell is made up of 2 matching B pieces and 2 contrasting A pieces. It's important to lay out the whole quilt before sewing because the A pieces must match the B pieces in the row above.

Begin laying out the pieces for the top row (Row A) with a pair of matching B pieces. Follow with another pair of matching B pieces and continue in this manner until you have laid out 5 pairs. Add a B piece to both ends of the row. Fill in each of the spaces between the B pieces with contrasting A pieces. Notice the A pieces that touch each other match. You should have 12 A pieces in the row. **2A**

The second row (Row B) begins with a matching pair of B pieces and is made up of 6 pairs across. The spaces between the B pieces are filled in with A pieces. Not only do these A pieces match each other, they also match the B pieces in the row above. **2B**

The third row (Row C) is made the same as Row A with one exception. The A pieces that touch each other between the B pieces also match the B pieces they touch in the row above. **2C**

Rows 2, 4, 6, 8, 10, 12, and 14 are all made like Row B.

Rows 3, 5, 7, 9, 11, and 13 are all made like Row C.

Once all the rows have all been laid out and you are sure all the pieces match where they should, begin sewing the pieces into blocks. Pick up the first set of A/B pieces. Fold each piece in half on the diagonal and finger press to mark the midway point of each curved edge. Place the A piece on top of the B piece with right sides facing and finger pressed centers aligned. Pin at the center point and at both ends of the seam allowance. **2D**

Stitch the 2 pieces together along the curve using a ¼" seam allowance. Use your fingers to ease in any fullness around the curve and avoid stretching the fabric as you sew. Press the seam allowance toward the A piece. **2E**

After the 2 pieces have been stitched together into a block, put the block back into the same place from which you picked it up. Continue sewing the A/B pieces together until you reach the end of each row.

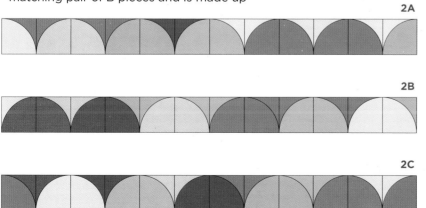

2A

2B

2C

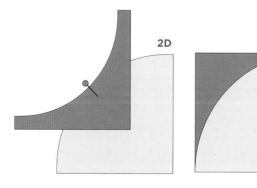

2D

2E

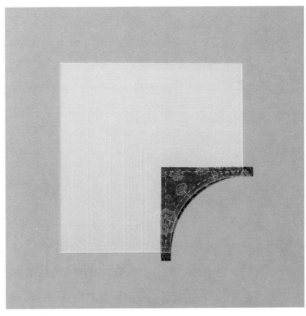

1 Select 2 matching 5″ print squares. Place template B on the lower right corner of each of the squares and cut around the curve.

2 After cutting the curve, align the 4½″ mark on Template A on the upper left corner of the square and cut the inner curve. After cutting the curve, align the 4½″ mark on Template A on the upper left corner of the square. Cut the inner curve and trim off both ends. Repeat for the matching square you selected. Keep all matching prints together!

3 Before sewing any pieces together, lay out all of the rows making sure all pieces match where they should. When you are happy with the layout, begin sewing the A and B pieces together by placing an A piece atop a B piece and pinning the 2 together at the midway point of the curve.

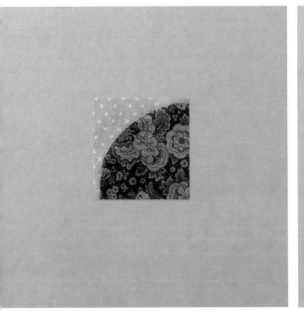

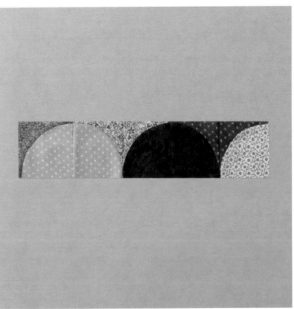

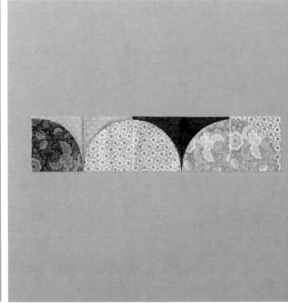

4 Press the seam allowance toward the A piece.

5 Row B begins with a matching pair of B pieces and is made up of 6 pairs across. The spaces between the B pieces are filled in with A pieces that match the B pieces in the row above.

6 The row that is beneath a B row uses A pieces that match the B pieces in the row above. By matching the A and B pieces from row to row, each clamshell unit will be complete.

After all the blocks have been made, sew each row together. It's a good idea to make sure all your matching pieces are still in place!

Sew all the rows together to complete the center of the quilt.

3 border

Cut (6) 6" strips across the width of the fabric. Sew the strips together end-to-end to make 1 long strip. Trim the borders from this strip.

Refer to Borders (pg. 102) in the Construction Basics to measure and cut the outer borders. The strips are approximately 56½" for the sides and approximately 59½" for the top and bottom.

4 quilt and bind

Layer the quilt with batting and backing and quilt. After the quilting is complete, square up the quilt and trim away all excess batting and backing. Add binding to complete the quilt. See Construction Basics (pg. 102) for binding instructions.

tilted nine-patch

I remember rides on the school bus fondly: Looking out the window as the streets passed by, my feet dangling down, chatting with my friends, and giggling when we'd hit a bump! My dear friend Cindy drove a school bus for a few years right before she got married, and she told me all about it. I can imagine riding on her bus would have been a lot of fun.

Cindy drove bus number 117. Each weekday morning, she woke up before sunrise to make sure her bus was in tiptop shape: peeking into the engine with a flashlight, knocking the tires with a small wooden club to check the pressure, and testing each of the emergency exits. She swept out the crumbs and papers left over from the previous day's rides. That bus was like a friend to her with its weathered brown seats, mint green interior, and booming horn. It was reliable and smooth on the road, taking wide turns with ease and stopping with a deep sigh, like a tired old man settling down into an easy chair.

Some days were incredibly trying for Cindy, some were affirming, and most were somewhere in between. Cindy loved talking and joking with students. She cherished their handwritten notes and wilted flowers. Working with children is different every day, and she was a positive influence in their lives, a constant they might not have had otherwise. It was amazing to her how a simple smile and kind "Hello" could

For the tutorial and everything you need to make this quilt visit: **www.msqc.co/blocksummer19**

change a student's day. She didn't know what she was taking on when she started driving a school bus, but it became so much more than moving students from point A to point B.

The last day of school would also be Cindy's last time on the bus, and she couldn't believe how quickly the years had passed. She'd been driving for more than two school years and was moving on to new adventures. The kids were bound to be filled with excitement, and so was she, but as she drove the empty bus to her first stop of the day, she couldn't help feeling nostalgic. If someone had told her when she was younger that she'd be a bus driver one day, she wouldn't have believed them, but the job came at a time when she needed it and it was eye-opening. As the last day progressed, and students got on and off the bus, Cindy's heart was filled to the brim. Some passed her handwritten notes and called out sincere goodbyes, and some leapt off the last step, running home without a glance backward, but she smiled during the whole ride, knowing she would miss even the most rowdy kids who always stood up before the bus had stopped!

As the students exited her school bus for the last time before summer break, Cindy handed them a sweet treat and wished them a happy summer. Then she parked her old bus, swept it out for the last time, shut the door, and continued on her journey.

materials

QUILT SIZE
71" x 71"

BLOCK SIZE
10" finished

QUILT TOP
1 roll 2½" print strips
1 roll 2½" background strips

BORDER
1¼ yards

BINDING
¾ yard

BACKING
4½ yards - vertical seam(s)

SAMPLE QUILT
Imperial Collection 15 by Studio RK for
Robert Kaufman

1 cut

From the background strips, cut:

- 27 strips into 2½" squares. Each
  strip will yield 16 squares and a **total
  of 432** are needed.

- Cut 9 strips into 2½" x 4½"
  rectangles. Each strip will yield 8
  rectangles and a **total of 72** are
  needed. Set the remaining strips
  aside for another project.

Select 36 strips from the roll of print
strips. Cut:

- (4) 2½" x 4½" rectangles from each
  strip. Set the remainder of each strip
  aside for the moment.

2 make 9-patch blocks

Pick up the strips you set aside. Select
3 contrasting strips and sew them
together along the length to make a
strip set. Press all seam allowances
in the same direction. Make 12 strip
sets and cut each into 2½" x 6½"
rectangles. Each strip set will yield
9 rectangles and a **total of 108** are
needed. **2A**

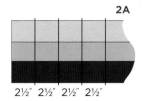

2A

2½" 2½" 2½" 2½"

Select 3 strip set rectangles. Sew them together to make a 9-patch block as shown. **Make 36. 2B**

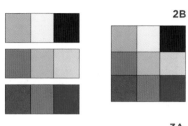

2B

3 make flying geese

To make each flying geese, pick up (2) 2½" background squares. Draw a line from corner to corner once on the diagonal to mark a sewing line on the reverse side of the squares. Place a marked square atop 1 end of a 2½" x 4½" print rectangle with right sides facing. Sew on the drawn line, then trim the excess fabric away ¼" from the sewn seam. Repeat for the other end of the print rectangle. Add a 2½" background square to the left of each flying geese to complete the unit. **Make 144. 3A**

3A

4 block construction

Sew a 2½" x 4½" background rectangle to the right of 2 of the flying geese units to make the top and bottom row of the block. **4A**

Make the center row of the block by sewing a flying geese unit to either side of the 9-patch block as shown. **4B**

Sew the 3 rows together to complete 1 block. **4C**

Make 36 blocks.

Block Size: 10" finished

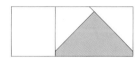

4A

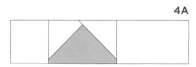

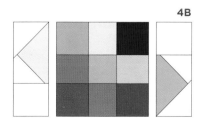

4B

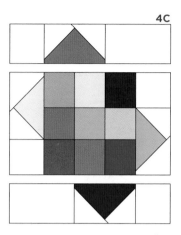

4C

5 arrange and sew

Lay out the blocks in rows. Each row is made up of **6 blocks** and **6 rows** are needed. Be aware of how each block is oriented as it is placed in the row. Refer to the diagram on page 37, if necessary. After the blocks have been sewn into rows, press the seam allowances of the odd rows toward the right and the even rows toward the left to make the seams nest.

Sew the rows together to complete the center of the quilt.

6 border

Cut (7) 6" strips across the width of the fabric. Sew the strips together end-to-end to make 1 long strip. Trim the borders from this strip.

1 Sew 3 contrasting 2½" print strips together along the length to make a strip set. Make 12 and cut each strip set into 2½" x 6½" rectangles.

2 Select 3 strip set rectangles and sew them into a 9-patch as shown.

3 Mark a sewing line once on the diagonal on the reverse side of (2) 2½" background squares. Place a marked square atop 1 end of a print rectangle with right sides facing. Sew on the line, trim the excess fabric away. Repeat for the other end.

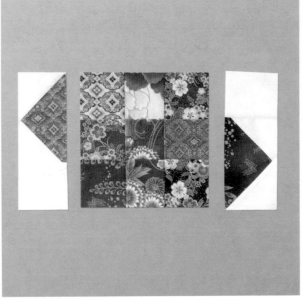

4 After adding a 2½" background square to the left of the flying geese unit, sew a 2½" x 4½" background rectangle to the right of the flying geese to make the top and bottom row of the block.

5 Sew a flying geese unit to either side of a 9-patch to make the center row of the block.

6 Sew the 3 rows together as shown to complete the block.

Refer to Borders (pg. 102) in the Construction Basics to measure and cut the outer borders. The strips are approximately 60½" for the sides and approximately 71½" for the top and bottom.

7 quilt and bind

Layer the quilt with batting and backing and quilt. After the quilting is complete, square up the quilt and trim away all excess batting and backing. Add binding to complete the quilt. See Construction Basics (pg. 102) for binding instructions.

For the tutorial and everything you need to make this quilt visit:
www.msqc.co/blocksummer19

turnabout
granny squares

Sightseeing in rural America is sure full of surprises! You never know what you might find around the next bend. Maybe the world's largest ball of string? Cars stacked to resemble Stonehenge? Or a palace built entirely out of corn? From coast to coast, there are plenty of sights worth stopping for, and here in Hamilton we have a new tourist attraction especially for quilters!

Thanks to the Redford family, sitting in the center of our town is the World's Largest Spool of Thread! Standing at 22 feet tall and 8 feet wide, wrapped with over 1 million yards of Aurifil thread, it's another great reason to come visit. So, how did this giant spool come to be? I talked with Dakota Redford to get the inside scoop.

Where did the idea for the world's largest spool of thread come from?
"Ryan's brain just kind of works that way. He thought it would be cool to have a tourist attraction where everyone would stop and take pictures"

How did you start planning to build the spool?
"Larry Richerson brought his vision to life. When Larry had put together the main beam and outside rings, in 'go big or go home' fashion, the center spike was 22 feet long!"

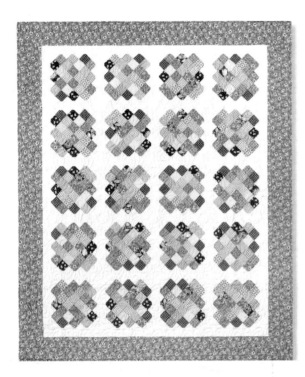

What challenges did you encounter?

"Winding it with thread! It would have been easier if the spool could spin, however, we laid it on its side and hand spooled all one million yards! Our family would spend a few hours each day handing the smaller spools of thread, over and under. Then we recruited about 10 volunteers from the community to assist."

How long did it take to build?

"Larry spent roughly a month to mold and weld the steel before it was ready to be painted."

How did Aurifil get involved?

"Karen Miller was an instructor during Missouri Star Academy. During a conversation with her, Ryan mentioned his idea for the World's Largest Spool. Karen is an Aurifilosopher, working for Aurifil to teach others about thread. She mentioned that Aurifil would love to help out. A few emails later we got the question that we were a little afraid to answer: 'How much thread do you need?' With our calculations we needed a million yards just to cover the core. We decided to shoot for the moon and asked for the million. Not a week later a box arrived on the porch with spool after spool of beautiful Aurifil thread!"

How long did it take to wind?

"Roughly 250 hours." That's over ten days of hard work!

Can people add on to it?

"Yes, absolutely! One of our favorite things is to drive by the spool to see someone adding their own thread. Find a place to tie on and go for it! And, often you can stop by and find a small spool of Aurifil thread sitting on the lip of the base waiting for the next person to add it! We look forward to seeing it grow over the years."

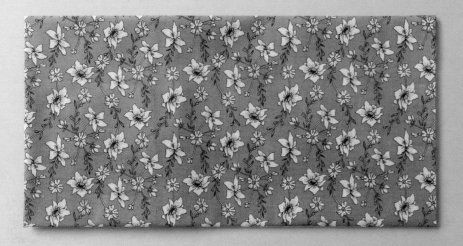

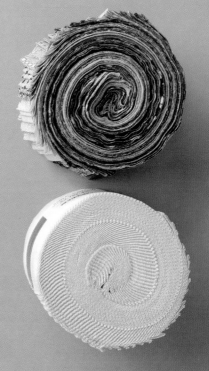

materials

QUILT SIZE
65" x 78"

BLOCK SIZE
11" finished

QUILT TOP
1 roll 2½" print strips
1 roll 2½" background strips - includes
    inner border

OUTER BORDER
1¼ yards

BINDING
¾ yard

BACKING
4¾ yards - vertical seam(s)

SAMPLE QUILT
Sweet Stems by Sue Daley Designs for
Riley Blake Designs

1 cut

Cut 5 background strips into 2½" x
11½" rectangles. Each strip will yield
3 rectangles and a **total of 15** are
needed. Set the rectangles aside for
vertical sashing rectangles. Set aside
(1) 2½" x 5½" scrap to add to the strips
used for horizontal sashing.

2 make strip sets

Strip Set A

Using scant ¼" seam allowances, sew
3 print strips together along the length
of the strips. Add a background strip
to the bottom to complete the set.
Make 5. Press the seam allowances

toward the top of the strip set. Cut
each strip set into 2½" increments.
Each strip set will yield 16 rectangles.
Stack all A rectangles together. **2A**

Strip Set B

Using scant ¼" seam allowances, sew
2 print strips together along the length
of the strips. Add a background strip,
then a print to complete the set. **Make
5.** Press the seam allowances toward
the bottom of the strip set. Cut each

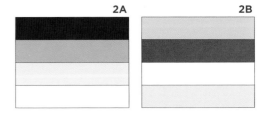

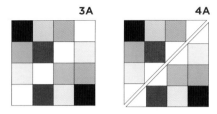

3A　　**4A**

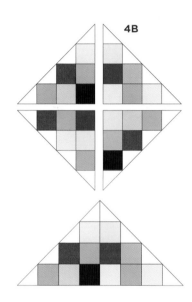

4B

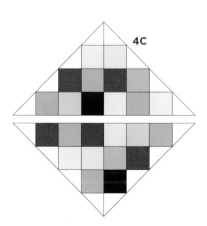

4C

strip set into 2½" increments. Each strip set will yield 16 rectangles. Stack all B rectangles together. **2B**

3 make 16-patch blocks

Select 2 A rectangles and 2 B rectangles. Continue to use scant ¼" seam allowances and sew 2 A rectangles and 2 B rectangles together as shown to make a 16-patch block. Notice that an A rectangle and a B rectangle have been turned 180° as they've been sewn in place. **Make 40. 3A**

4 block construction

Cut each of the 16-patch blocks in half on the diagonal. Notice that we are always cutting through the background squares. Each half of a 16-patch block makes up 1 quadrant of the completed Granny Square block. **4A**

Select 4 quadrants that don't match from the cut 16-patches. Turn each quadrant of the block so the white pieces are on the outer edge of the block. Using a scant ¼" seam allowance, sew 2 quadrants together to make 1 half of the block. Make 2 halves. **4B**

Sew the 2 halves together, still using a scant ¼" seam allowance, to complete the block.
Make 20 blocks. **4C**
Block Size: 11" finished

5 arrange and sew

Pick up the (15) 2½" x 11½" background rectangles you set aside earlier. Lay out the blocks in **5 rows of 4** and add a 2½" x 11½" sashing rectangle between each block. Sew each row together. *Notice as you are sewing that all outer points of the block become incorporated into the seam allowances.* Press all seam allowances toward the sashing rectangles.

Make horizontal sashing strips by sewing 5 background 2½" x width of fabric strips together end-to-end. Add the 2½" x 5½" scrap that was set aside earlier. Subcut the strip into (4) 2½" x 50½" strips.

Sew the rows together adding a horizontal sashing strip between each row to complete the center of the quilt.
Again, notice that all outer points of the block become incorporated into the seam allowances.

6 inner border

Pick up (6) 2½" x width of fabric background strips. Sew the strips together end-to-end to make 1 long strip. Trim the borders from this strip.

Refer to Borders (pg. 102) in the Construction Basics to measure and cut the inner borders. The strips are

1 Make strip set A by sewing 3 print strips and 1 background strip together along the length of the strips using a scant ¼″ seam allowance. Make sure the strips are placed in the order shown.

2 Make strip set B by sewing 3 print strips and 1 background strip together along the length of the strips using a scant ¼″ seam allowance. Notice the order of the strips has changed. The background strip is now the second strip from the bottom.

3 After cutting all strip sets into 2½″ rectangles, select 2 A rectangles and 2 B rectangles. Sew the rectangles together to make a 16-patch block as shown. Notice that an A rectangle and a B rectangle have been turned 180° as they've been sewn together.

4 Cut each of the 16-patch blocks in half on the diagonal. Notice that we are always cutting through the background squares. Each half of a 16-patch block makes up 1 quadrant of the completed Granny Square block.

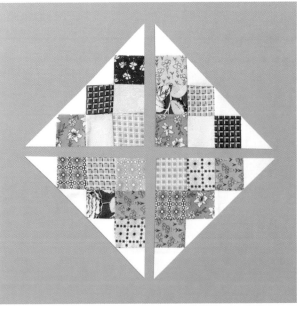

5 Select 4 quadrants that don't match from the cut 16-patches. Turn each quadrant of block until the background pieces all face the outer edge of the block.

6 Sew the quadrants together as shown using a scant ¼″ seam allowance to complete the block.

approximately 63½″ for the sides and approximately 54½″ for the top and bottom.

7 outer border

Cut (7) 6″ strips across the width of the fabric. Sew the strips together end-to-end to make 1 long strip. Trim the borders from this strip.

Refer to Borders (pg. 102) in the Construction Basics to measure and cut the outer borders. The strips are approximately 67½″ for the sides and approximately 65½″ for the top and bottom.

8 quilt and bind

Layer the quilt with batting and backing and quilt. After the quilting is complete, square up the quilt and trim away all excess batting and backing. Add binding to complete the quilt. See Construction Basics (pg. 102) for binding instructions.

leafy tree tops
table runner

Girls' Camp was a yearly tradition when I was young. It was a week of sleeping in creaky cabins, hiking in the forest, cooking over campfires, and singing nonstop! I adored my time at camp, but for my young friend, Alice, camp was her least favorite thing on earth.

As soon as Alice set foot in her cabin, she was sure she'd have a bad time at camp. It smelled like bug spray and someone had spilled a large thermos of Kool-Aid on the floor, attracting mosquitos from the furthest reaches of the lake. She sat heavily on her bunk and sighed. Camp was going to stink, literally.

The name of Alice's cabin group was the "Sunflowers." The campers were given vests with large, yellow craft-store sunflowers glued onto them, and even their hats were embellished with the tacky flowers. She refused to put the hat on; the vest was enough humiliation.

The leaders seemed to be as chipper as can be, singing bright and early in the morning and skipping around in their hiking boots. As Alice unpacked her bag, she frowned, wishing she could go home. That morning during roll call at the flagpole, the rules of camp were announced. One of them piqued her interest: "Any girl who jumps off the waterfall will be sent home." Really? Sent home? That could be it! All she had to do was muster up her courage and jump, then she wouldn't have to live out this week-long torture.

For the tutorial and everything you need to make this quilt visit: **www.msqc.co/blocksummer19**

During free time, Alice surveyed the lake and the waterfall. It was high, about 30 feet up. She gulped. As she paddled around near the dock in a large inner tube, she overheard some of her campmates chatting and found that a few of them had been intrigued by the waterfall as well. They whispered amongst themselves, creating a plan. Alice admired their bravery, wondering if she could ever take the plunge herself.

By the next day, the Sunflowers' plan was fully formed. Every single girl in the cabin had heard about the waterfall pact and they were all going to jump. Alice plotted along with them. It turned out that these girls weren't quite the goody-two-shoes they had seemed on the first day. They soon formed an alliance, ranging throughout camp causing low-level mayhem. For example, any camper caught entering a porta-potty without posting a lookout might find themselves being rocked from side to side by the Sunflowers as soon as the door was closed!

With only a couple days left of camp, the girls ventured up to the waterfall. Standing on the edge, with the water rushing down, Alice's nerves almost got the best of her, but then someone started counting, "One, two, three ... jump!" They held hands and jumped. She fell for a long moment and hit the water with a giant splash. The girls glanced around quickly at each other, everyone bobbed up out of the water and they all let out a cheer! Guess who was getting sent home from camp?

Nobody. Because their entire cabin had jumped, the leaders decided that they couldn't possibly send everyone home. By then, Alice had started smiling. She didn't know it, but the next four summers spent at Girls' Camp would be the best ones of her life.

materials

TABLE RUNNER SIZE
24" x 54"

BLOCK SIZE
6" finished

TABLE RUNNER TOP
1 package of 5" print squares
¾ yard background fabric-includes
    inner border

OUTER BORDER
½ yard

BINDING
½ yard

BACKING
1¾ yards - horizontal seam(s)

SAMPLE QUILT
Artisan Batiks Round and Around
by Lunn Studios for Robert Kaufman

1 cut

Select 24 print 5" squares. Cut each in half vertically and horizontally to make 2½" squares. Each square will yield 4 squares and each block uses 4 matching squares of 1 print and 3 matching squares of a second print.

Select 4 print 5" squares that complement the pieces you are using to make the leaves. Cut (3) 1½" x 4" rectangles from each square.

From 1 print square, cut (3) 1½" squares.

From the background fabric, cut:

- (2) 1½" strips across the width of the fabric – subcut each strip into (6) 1½" x 6½" rectangles for a **total of 12**.

- (9) 2½" strips across the width of the fabric – subcut 4 strips into (16) 2½" squares and (1) strip into (8) 2½" squares for a **total of 72**. Subcut 2 strips into (1) 2½" x 13½" rectangle and (1) 2½" x 17½" rectangles. Set aside the (2) 2½" x 17½" rectangles, the 2 remaining strips as well as the rest of the strip from which the (8) 2½" squares were cut. These pieces will be used when making the inner border.

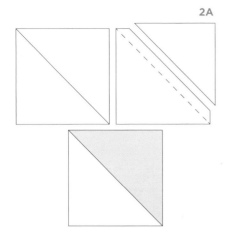

2A

2 block construction

To make half-square triangle units, pick up 4 matching 2½" print squares and 4 background 2½" squares. Draw a line once on the diagonal on the reverse side of the background squares. Place a marked background square atop a print square and sew on the marked line. Trim the excess fabric ¼" away from the sewn seam. Open and press the seam allowance toward the darker fabric. Make 4 and set aside for the moment. **2A**

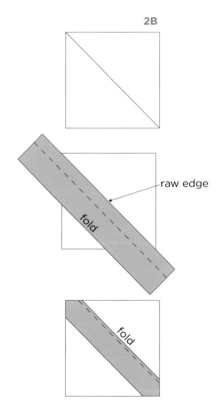

2B

raw edge

fold

fold

Choose a 1½" x 4" complementary rectangle and a 2½" background square. Press the background square in half on the diagonal. Press the rectangle in half lengthwise with wrong sides facing. Open the pressed background square and align the long raw edges of the print rectangle along the crease on the right side of the background square. Stitch the rectangle to the background square using a ¼" seam allowance. Fold the rectangle back over, covering the seam allowance and top stitch along the pressed edge. Trim the edges of the rectangle evenly with the background square to complete the stem unit. **2B**

Lay out the half-square triangle units, a stem unit, 1 background square and 3 print 2½" squares in rows as shown. **2C**

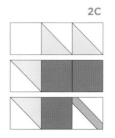

2C

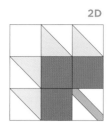

2D

Sew the pieces together to make the 3 rows, then sew the rows together to complete 1 leaf block. **Make 12. 2D**

Block Size: 6" finished

3 arrange and sew

Lay out the leaf blocks in **6 rows of 2**, paying particular attention to the direction the blocks are placed. Add a 1½" x 6½" background rectangle between each leaf. Make a narrow horizontal sashing strip by sewing a 1½" x 6½" background rectangle to a 1½" print square. Make 3 narrow horizontal sashing strips. Place each strip between 2 sashed leaf units as shown. **3A**

Place a 2½" x 13½" sashing strip between each set of 4 leaves. Sew all rows together to complete the center of the table runner. **3B**

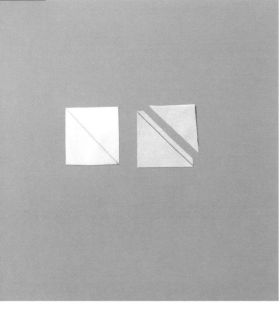

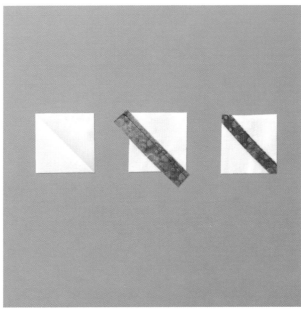

1 Make half-square triangle units. Draw a line once on the diagonal on the reverse side of the 2½" background triangles. Place a marked square atop a print square and sew on the line. Trim the excess fabric ¼" away from the sewn seam. Press the seam allowance toward the darker fabric.

2 Choose a 1½" x 4" complementary rectangle and a 2½" background square. Press the square in half on the diagonal. Press the rectangle in half lengthwise with wrong sides facing. Align the edges of the rectangle along the crease on the background square. Stitch in place. Flip the rectangle over the seam allowance and top stitch along the pressed edge.

3 Sew 2 matching half-square triangle units to a 2½" background square to make the top row. Sew a half-square triangle unit to (2) 2½" matching print squares to make the center row. Sew a half-square triangle to a 2½" square. Add a stem unit to complete the bottom row.

4 Sew the 3 rows together to complete the block.

5 Select 4 blocks. Sew 1 to either side of a 1½" x 6½" background rectangle. Make 2 rows in this manner as shown. Sew a 1½" x 6½" background rectangle to either side of a 1½" square. Sew the 3 rows together.

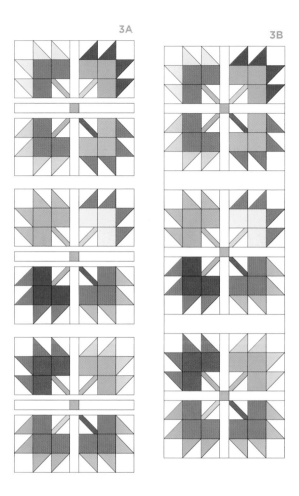

3A   3B

5 outer border

Cut (4) 4″ strips across the width of the fabric.
Sew the strips together end-to-end to make 1
long strip. Trim the borders from this strip.

Refer to Borders (pg. 102) in the Construction
Basics to measure and cut the outer borders.
The strips are approximately 47½″ for the sides
and approximately 24½″ for the top and bottom.

6 quilt and bind

Layer the table runner with batting and backing
and quilt. After the quilting is complete, square it
up and trim away all excess batting and backing.
Add binding to complete the table runner.
See Construction Basics (pg. 102) for binding
instructions.

4 inner border

Pick up the background pieces that were set
aside earlier for the inner border. Set aside the
(2) 2½″ x 17½″ rectangles for the moment. Sew
the remaining strips together to make 1 long
strip. Trim the side inner borders from this
strip. The strips are approximately 43½″. Sew
1 to each side of the table runner. Add a 2½″ x
17½″ rectangle to each end. If you need help
on how to measure and cut borders, refer to
Borders (pg. 102) in the Construction Basics.

*For the tutorial and everything
you need to make this quilt visit:*
www.msqc.co/blocksummer19

may day
baskets

It's that time of year. The kids are out of school! But how can we keep them occupied? I can picture it now: A humid house filled with lethargic children, sprawled on the couch, moaning and groaning about how bored they are! Well, in my opinion, the best cure for boredom is curiosity. Get those kids reading and summer will fly right by!

Local libraries across the country are gearing up for summer reading programs as we speak. These fantastic programs came from the fact that after school is over, children regress during the summer months, especially in reading. As the school years progress, summer reading loss can really add up. Faithful librarians are teaming up with schools and parents to provide opportunities for kids to keep their love of reading alive during the summer.

Instilling a love of reading in children can be a bit of a challenge. Not every child has access to a wide variety of books at home. It's hard for them to feel a desire to read when they don't have books they identify with. As J.K. Rowling said, "If you don't like to read, you haven't found the right book." Libraries are wonderful for providing an incredible array of options. And once they latch onto a new favorite, get out of the way because it's hard to separate a kid from a good book, even when it's dinnertime!

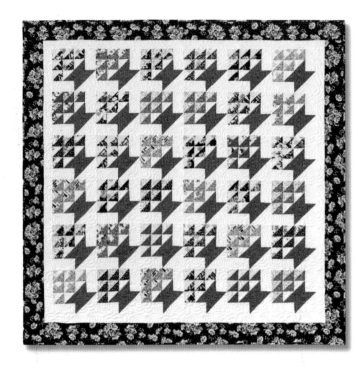

Summer reading programs have so much to explore. They offer a wide selection of great books to choose from and they also include fun activities that go a step beyond, engaging children as they read and rewarding their efforts. All libraries offer different rewards, but the Hamilton local library has prizes ranging from bubbles and sidewalk chalk to toy cars and even Kindle tablets! Kids sign up in mid-May and the program starts in June. The children meet with the librarian and make a goal for how many books or minutes they want to read during the summer and then check in weekly for prizes, but the real reward is the fun they'll have discovering new books they love!

You may be wondering how to keep the momentum going once summer is over. Do things to make reading special! I used to tell my kids to get lost with a book. Go anywhere in the house and snuggle up. And they got creative! I'd find them on the stairs, in the bathtub with a blanket, inside the closet, under the dining room table, and up in trees. It doesn't matter where you read, but my favorite place was always under the covers with a flashlight.

This summer, when you hear those familiar moans and groans, take a much-needed trip to your local library. Bring home the biggest stack of books you can manage, and spend those long summer days reading in your favorite spot. There's no need to hit the road for a vacation. Each book contains a world of its own. As Dr. Seuss famously said, "The more that you read, the more things you will know. The more you learn, the more places you'll go."

materials

QUILT SIZE
73" x 73"

BLOCK SIZE
10" finished

QUILT TOP
1 roll 2½" print strips
2½ yards background fabric-includes
    inner border
1 yard complementary print fabric

OUTER BORDER
1¼ yards

BINDING
¾ yard

BACKING
4½ yards - vertical seam(s)

OTHER
Clearly Perfect Slotted Trimmers

SAMPLE QUILT
Field Day by Kelly Ventura for
Windham Fabrics

1 cut

From the background fabric, cut:

• (12) 2½" strips across the width of the
  fabric. Set 7 strips aside for the inner
  border.

• (11) 3" strips across the width of
  the fabric – subcut 10 strips into
  3" x 5½" rectangles. Each strip will
  yield 7 rectangles. Subcut (2) 3" x
  5½" rectangles from the last strip
  and add them to the ones you have
  already cut. You will have a **total of 72**
  rectangles.

• (3) 6" strips across the width of the
  fabric – subcut each strip into (6) 6"
  squares. Each strip will yield 6 squares
  and a **total of 18** are needed.

From the complementary fabric, cut:

• (5) 2½" strips across the width of the
  fabric.

• (3) 6" strips across the width of the
  fabric – subcut each strip into (6) 6"
  squares. Each strip will yield 6 squares
  and a **total of 18** are needed.

2 small half-square triangles

Select 18 light to medium 2½" print
strips from the roll and 18 dark 2½" print
strips. Pair a light or medium print strip
with a dark print strip and layer the 2
strips together with right sides facing.
Sew on both lengths of the strips using
a ¼" seam allowance. You will have a
tube after sewing the 2 seams. Make a
total of 18 tubes. **2A**

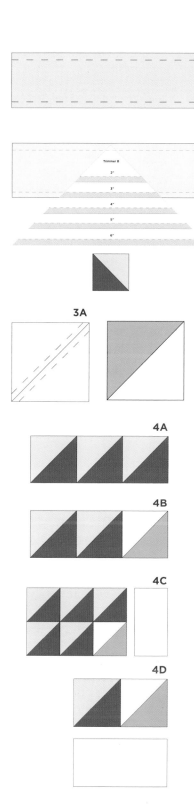

2A

2B

3A

4A

4B

4C

4D

Use the Clearly Perfect Slotted Trimmer B triangle when cutting the pieces for the half-square triangles. Align the dotted 3″ mark on the seam line of the tube. Cut along the 2 edges of the ruler. While you're in the process of trimming, use the slots provided to trim off the dog ears. Flip the ruler 180°, again aligning the 3″ dotted mark on the seam line and the angle along the edge you have just cut. Cut on the angle, then use the slots provided to trim off the dog ears. Continue cutting in this manner until you have cut 12 half-square triangles from each tube. Each block requires 6 matching half-square triangle units, and a **total of 216** are needed for the quilt.

Open and press each half-square triangle with the seam allowance toward the darker fabric. Keep all matching half-square triangles together. **2B**

Note: You can cut 16 half-square triangles from each tube. If you prefer, you can cut half-square triangles all the way across each tube and set the extras aside for another project.

Pick up the (5) 2½″ background strips and the (5) 2½″ complementary print strips. Repeat the previous instructions and make a **total of 5** tubes and use the trimmer to cut 16 half-square triangles from each tube. Each block requires 2 matching half-square triangle units, and a **total of 72** are needed for the quilt. Keep all matching half-square triangles together.

3 large half-square triangles

On the reverse side of the (18) 6″ background squares, draw a line from corner to corner once on the diagonal. Layer a marked 6″ background square with a 6″ complementary print square

with right sides facing. Sew on both sides of the drawn line using a ¼″ seam allowance. Cut on the drawn line, and square up each half-square triangle to 5½″ using the Clearly Perfect Slotted Trimmer A triangle. Open each and press the seam allowance toward the darkest fabric. Each square will yield 2 half-square triangles and a **total of 36** are needed. **3A**

4 block construction

Select 6 matching half-square triangle units and 2 matching complementary print half-square triangle units. Add (2) 3″ x 5½″ background rectangles to the stack, as well as 1 large complementary half-square triangle.

Sew 3 of the matching half-square triangle units together to make 1 row. **4A**

Sew 2 matching half-square triangles units and 1 complementary print half-square triangle unit together to make another row. **4B**

Sew the two rows together and add a 3″ x 5½″ background rectangle as shown. Set aside for the moment. **4C**

Stitch the remaining matching half-square triangle unit to the remaining complementary print half-square triangle unit. Sew a 3″ x 5½″ background rectangle to the bottom of the two. **4D**

Add the large half-square triangle to the end. **4E**

You now have 2 rows. Sew the 2 rows together to complete the block. **Make 36** blocks. **4F**

Block Size: 10″ finished

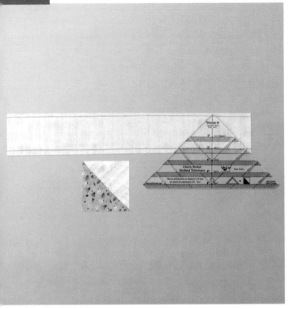

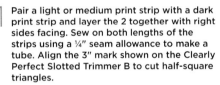

1 Pair a light or medium print strip with a dark print strip and layer the 2 together with right sides facing. Sew on both lengths of the strips using a ¼" seam allowance to make a tube. Align the 3" mark shown on the Clearly Perfect Slotted Trimmer B to cut half-square triangles.

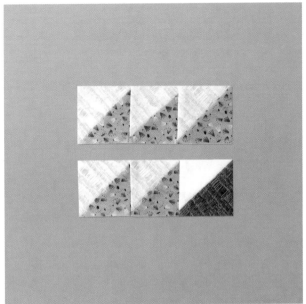

2 Make the top row of the basket by sewing 3 matching half-square triangles together as shown. Row 2 is made by sewing 2 matching half-square triangles together and adding a third half-square triangle unit made of background and complementary fabric.

3 Sew the first and second rows together, then add a 3" x 5½" background rectangle to the right. This is the top portion of the basket. Set aside for the moment.

4 Sew the remaining matching half-square triangle unit to the remaining complementary print half-square triangle unit. Add a 3" x 5½" background rectangle to the bottom.

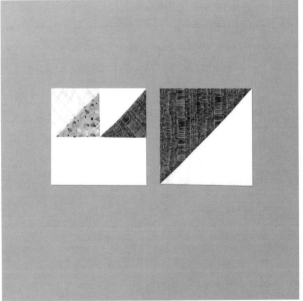

5 Add a large half-square triangle unit to the end of the 2 rows to complete the bottom portion of the basket.

6 Sew the top and the bottom portions of the basket together to complete the block.

4E

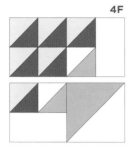

4F

5 arrange and sew

Lay out the blocks in rows. Each row is made up of **6 blocks** and **6 rows** are needed. After the blocks have been sewn into rows, press the seam allowances of the odd-numbered rows toward the right and the even-numbered rows toward the left to make the seams nest.

Sew the rows together to complete the center of the quilt.

6 inner border

Pick up the 7 strips you set aside for the inner border. Sew the strips together end-to-end to make one long strip. Trim the borders from this strip.

Refer to Borders (pg. 102) in the Construction Basics to measure and cut the inner borders. The strips are approximately 60½" for the sides and approximately 64½" for the top and bottom.

7 outer border

Cut (7) 5" strips across the width of the fabric. Sew the strips together end-to-end to make 1 long strip. Trim the borders from this strip.

Refer to Borders (pg. 102) in the Construction Basics to measure and cut the outer borders. The strips are approximately 64½" for the sides and approximately 73½" for the top and bottom.

8 quilt and bind

Layer the quilt with batting and backing and quilt. After the quilting is complete, square up the quilt and trim away all excess batting and backing. Add binding to complete the quilt. See Construction Basics (pg. 102) for binding instructions.

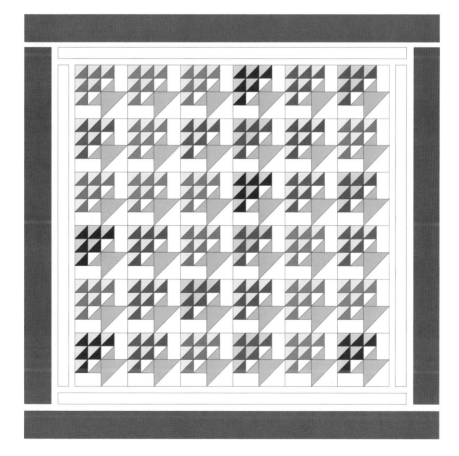

rickrack

The kids in Mrs. Brown's 6th grade class were excited to graduate elementary school and move on to junior high, but there was a sense of melancholy, too. Mrs. Brown was unlike any teacher they had ever known. It would be hard to leave her behind.

She was 63 years old—almost old enough to retire—yet she had a way of connecting with children that made those years practically melt away. She was wise and strict with discipline, but she treated her students with respect. She expected them to act grown-up, and so, for the most part, they did.

She joked with them and trusted them. She challenged them and gave them the confidence they needed to learn. After a full school year of being carefully tended and nurtured, the kids of room 103 had grown in ways that simply can't be measured by year-end testing.

As the last day of school drew near, the kids started whispering among themselves out on the playground. Mrs. Brown had been so good to them; she had become their friend. Now, they wanted to say goodbye with a bang!

Like many women of her generation, Mrs. Brown had a very carefully-tended hairstyle. It was painstakingly curled and sprayed once a week. Of course, the children knew nothing about hairdos, and so they planned and plotted what was sure to be the best send-off ever.

"Come out to the playground, Mrs. Brown!" the children coaxed on the last day of school. "We have a surprise for you!" They led her to a chair under one of the big Sycamore trees on the playground and hastily tied a handkerchief over her eyes.

For the tutorial and everything you need to make this quilt visit:
www.msqc.co/blocksummer19

Noelle Stevensen crept up behind Mrs. Brown with a water bucket in her hands. She held her finger to her lips, reminding the other children to keep quiet. "Okay! You can take off the blindfold!"

Mrs. Brown noticed the first water balloon one instant before it exploded on her left knee. Then another. Then another. Kids were hurling balloons from every direction, and in mere moments, she was soaked! Just when it seemed the supply of balloons had been exhausted, Noelle lifted that bucket high and poured it all out, right on Mrs. Brown's head!

Her silver hair lay wet and limp against her forehead. Mascara dripped down her cheeks. Her new teal sweater set hung from her shoulders, as wet as if she had jumped off the high dive into a swimming pool.

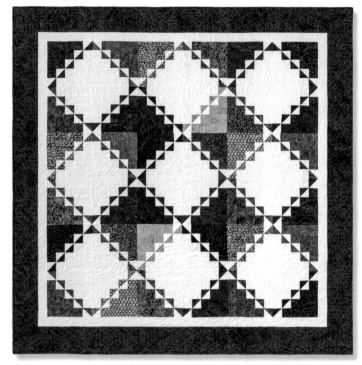

She sat in stunned silence, staring out at her giggling students as if from behind a window. They were wild with excitement, laughing and pointing and reenacting the entire ambush.

Neil was the first one to notice Mrs. Brown's startled expression. "Wait guys! Wait! I don't think she liked it!" In an instant, giggles turned to silence, then a rush of apologies. "Mrs. Brown! We didn't mean it!" "It was just for fun!"

Out of the corner of her eye, Mrs. Brown noticed a unscathed water balloon just within arms reach. She smiled, reached down to grab that balloon, and popped it right on Noelle's Stevenson's forehead! Everyone erupted in squeals of delight, declaring Mrs. Brown to be the most epic of all 6th grade teachers. It was a day to remember, for sure!

materials

QUILT SIZE
75" x 75"

BLOCK SIZE
10" finished

QUILT TOP
1 roll 2½" print strips
1 roll 2½" background strips

INNER BORDER
¼ yard

OUTER BORDER
1¼ yards

BINDING
¾ yard

BACKING
4¾ yards - vertical seam(s)

SAMPLE QUILT
Graphic Jewels Batiks by Kathy Engle
for Island Batiks

1 cut

Select 36 print strips from the roll. Cut each strip into the following increments:

- (6) 2½" squares
- (1) 2½" x 4½" rectangle
- (1) 2½" x 6½" rectangle
- (1) 2½" x 8½" rectangle

Keep all matching prints together.

Select 36 background strips. Cut each strip into the following increments and stack together by size:

- (6) 2½" squares
- (1) 2½" x 4½" rectangle
- (1) 2½" x 6½" rectangle
- (1) 2½" x 8½" rectangle

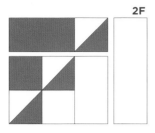

2F

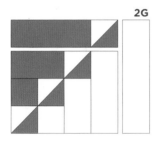

2G

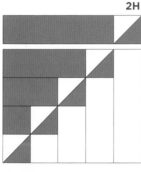

2H

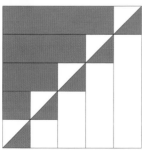

2 block construction

Make Half-Square Triangles

Pick up 5 print 2½" squares and 5 background 2½" squares. Mark a line from corner to corner once on the diagonal on the reverse side of each of the 5 background squares. Layer a marked background square with a print square. Sew on the line, then trim the excess fabric away ¼" from the sewn seam. Make 5 units. **2A**

Sew a half-square triangle unit to the 2½" print square and to each of the print rectangles. Notice that the background portion of the half-square triangle always touches the print. Press the seam allowance toward the print. Set aside for the moment. **2B**

Sew a half-square triangle unit to a 2½" background square as shown. Press the seam allowance toward the darkest fabric. **2C**

Pick up the smallest print/half-square triangle rectangle. Sew it to the half-square triangle/background strip to make a 4-patch as shown. **2D**

Stitch a background 2½" x 4½" rectangle to the side. **2E**

Add a print/half-square triangle rectangle next. Then add a 2½" x 6½" background rectangle as shown. **2F**

Add a print/half-square triangle rectangle next. Then add a 2½" x 8½" background rectangle as shown. **2G**

Complete the block by adding the remaining print/half-square triangle rectangle. **Make 36** blocks. **2H**

Block Size: 10" finished

3 arrange and sew

Lay out the blocks in rows paying particular attention to the way each block is positioned. Refer to the diagram on page 69, if necessary. Each row is made up of **6 blocks** and **6 rows** are needed. After the blocks have been sewn into rows, press the seam allowances of the odd-numbered rows toward the right and the even-numbered rows toward the left to make the seams nest.

Sew the rows together to complete the center of the quilt.

4 inner border

Cut (3) 2½" strips across the width of the background fabric. Add the 4 remaining background strips that are left from the roll. Sew the strips together end-to-end to make 1 long strip. Trim the borders from this strip.

Refer to Borders (pg. 102) in the Construction Basics to measure and cut the inner borders. The strips are approximately 60½" for the sides and

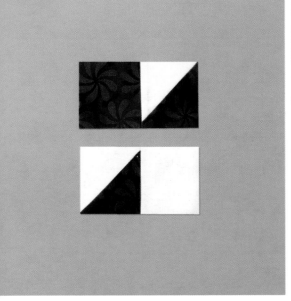

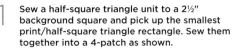

1 Sew a half-square triangle unit to a 2½″ background square and pick up the smallest print/half-square triangle rectangle. Sew them together into a 4-patch as shown.

2 Add a background 2½″ x 4½″ rectangle to the right as shown.

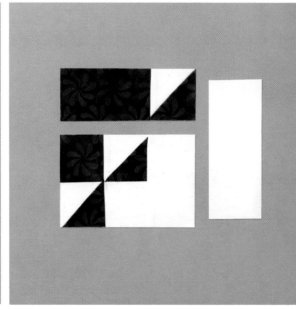

3 Add a 2½″ x 6½″ print/half-square triangle rectangle unit next. Then add a 2½″ x 6½″ background rectangle to the right.

4 Add a 2½″ x 8½″ print/half-square triangle rectangle unit next. Then add a 2½″ x 8½″ background rectangle as shown.

5 Add the remaining print/half-square triangle unit as shown to complete the block.

6 Make 36 blocks.

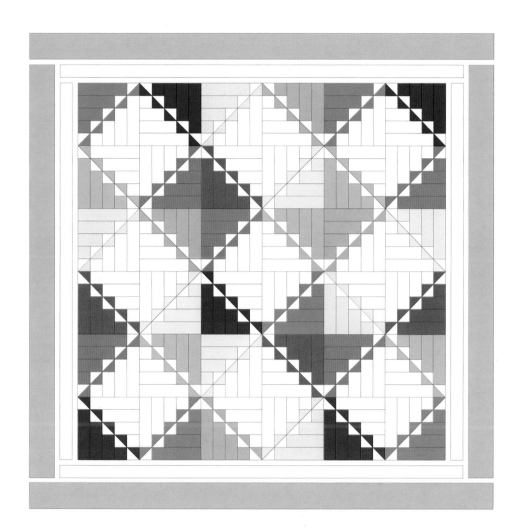

approximately 64½" for the top and bottom.

5 outer border

Cut (7) 6" strips across the width of the fabric. Sew the strips together end-to-end to make 1 long strip. Trim the borders from this strip.

Refer to Borders (pg. 102) in the Construction Basics to measure and cut the outer borders. The strips are approximately 64½" for the sides and approximately 75½" for the top and bottom.

6 quilt and bind

Layer the quilt with batting and backing and quilt. After the quilting is complete, square up the quilt and trim away all excess batting and backing. Add binding to complete the quilt. See Construction Basics (pg. 102) for binding instructions.

*For the tutorial and everything
you need to make this quilt visit:*

www.msqc.co/blocksummer19

berry
season

When you are young, staying cool on a hot day is easy as pie. A three-year-old child can strip down to their birthday suit and race through the sprinklers. Nobody bats an eye! They can splash all day in a four-foot kiddie pool. They can live on popsicles and snow cones morning, noon, and night.

But what about us grownups? Are we destined to languish in a sweaty heap all summer long? No! We just have to get a little creative! Here are a few options for staying cool as a cucumber as the temperatures soar:

Take in a show: Movie theaters are notoriously frigid, giving you a much-needed break from the heat.

Invest in a tiny phone fan: Did you know you can purchase cute little fans that attach to your smartphone? They plug into your charging port and provide quite the delightful icy blast. Find a shady spot to relax with your phone, and that trusty fan will keep a steady, cool breeze going as you enjoy Jenny's tutorials on the Quilting Tutorials app!

Go for a swim: Toss aside any reservations you may have; swimming is the ultimate cool-down, and it's great exercise, too! I have a friend in Las Vegas who can't miss her evening swim. "If

I don't go to the pool, I toss and turn all night; it's just too hot! But even a quick dip in the water cools me off and I sleep so much better!"

Eat a lot of ice cream: Trust me on this.

Head to the fabric store: The weather's always fine in between aisles of quilting cotton! (Bonus points if you make it all the way here to Missouri Star in Hamilton, Missouri! We've got 12 uniquely themed quilt shops all in a row! It takes just a few steps to get from batiks to florals to extra-wide backings, and you might run into Jenny while you're at it! Plus, we have a great, air-conditioned lounge for the non-quilters in your group. Go to visitmsqc.com to drool over photos of this quilter's dreamland!)

Take up ice skating: You'll feel like a magical ice fairy gliding across that frozen rink. Pro tip: Don't forget to bring your video recorder. If the skating trip doesn't go well, you might make millions off the bloopers!

Relocate your sewing room to the South Pole. It may seem like a labor-intensive venture, but just think! You could hire a crew of trained penguins to press your seams and sweep up thread scraps!

If all else fails, just remember: the lazy days of summer aren't called "lazy" for nothing! So kick back and enjoy some time with family, friends, and an issue of Block!

materials

QUILT SIZE
48" x 48"

BLOCK SIZE
3" x 3½" finished

QUILT TOP
2 packages 5" print squares
2 packages 5" background squares
¼ yard matching background fabric

BORDER
¾ yard

BINDING
½ yard

BACKING
3¼ yards - horizontal seam(s)

OTHER
Missouri Star Small Simple Wedge
Template

SAMPLE QUILT
Cinnaberry by 3 Sisters for
Moda Fabrics

1 cut

From the ¼ yard of background fabric,
cut:

- (6) 5" squares – add the squares to
  those in the 2 packages of precuts.

From each 5" square, cut:

- 2 triangles using the Small Simple
  Wedge Template. You will have a
  total of 168 print wedges and a **total
  of 180** background wedges. **1A**

2 arrange and sew

Lay out the wedges in rows. Each row
is made up of 15 background wedges

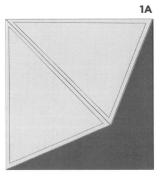

1A

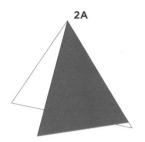

2A

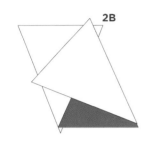

2B

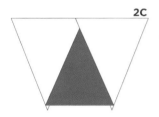

2C

and 14 print wedges. Each row begins and ends with a background wedge and alternates with a print wedge. Be aware of how the background wedges and the print wedges are oriented. **Make 12** rows.

Once you are satisfied with the layout, begin sewing the wedges together. As you sew 1 wedge to the next, be sure to offset the pieces by ¼". **2A 2B 2C**

After all the rows have been made, press the seam allowances toward the print wedges. Before sewing 1 row to the next, pin the 2 together, making sure the peaks of the triangles are aligned.

After the rows have been sewn together, trim the edges of both sides of the quilt, leaving a ¼" seam allowance. **2D**

3 border

Cut (5) 3½" strips across the width of the fabric. Sew the strips together end-to-end to make 1 long strip. Trim the borders from this strip.

Refer to Borders (pg. 102) in the Construction Basics to measure and cut the borders. The strips are approximately 42½" for the sides and approximately 48½" for the top and bottom.

4 quilt and bind

Layer the quilt with batting and backing and quilt. After the quilting is complete, square up the quilt and trim away all excess batting and backing. Add binding to complete the quilt. See Construction Basics (pg. 102) for binding instructions.

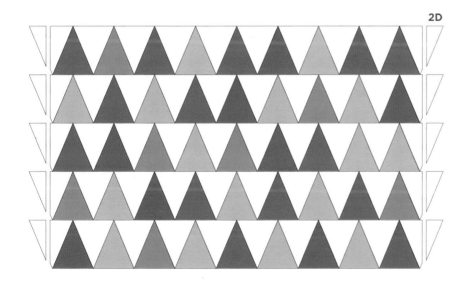

2D

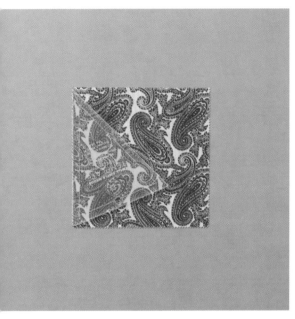

1 From each 5″ square, cut 2 wedges using the Small Simple Wedge template.

2 As 1 wedge is sewn to the next, the pieces are offset by ¼″.

3 Each row begins and ends with a background wedge and alternates with a print wedge. Align the peaks of the print wedges as the rows are sewn together.

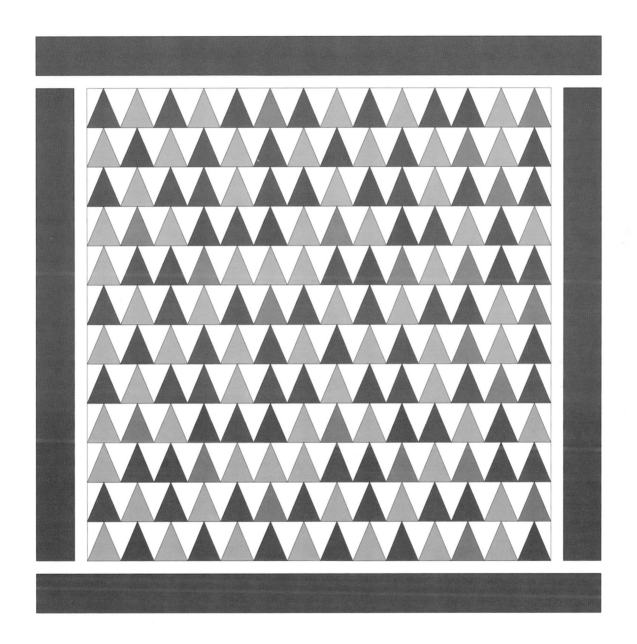

night sky

Isn't it funny how fast time seems to pass as you're growing up? When I was a kid, summer vacation seemed like a near-endless adventure. Three whole months until school starts again? I could do anything! Nowadays, it seems like I blink and my kids are all grown up, and when someone says "about 10 years ago," my brain still thinks 1995! At least we can look back at those long-lasting summers of childhood and remember when time moved a bit more like the tortoise than the hare. My friend, David, told me all about his nostalgic summertime adventures at the family farm:

"Growing up, summer vacations rarely had a routine for me; one year I would be traveling to a monument or museum, on another I would take trips to visit family or friends. My parents always tried to expose me to all kinds of experiences, rather than us sitting around the house all summer. But, there was always one constant to those summer breaks: Every July, no matter what my parents' work schedules were like or what trips they had planned, we would find ourselves down at the family farm."

"Just outside the tiny town of Sarcoxie in southern Missouri, my great-grandparents' farm was far away from anywhere that could be called 'bustling.' While no one lived on the land anymore, my grandfather and his brothers kept the fields and buildings maintained after they inherited it. There was one part, though, that remained untouched: a meandering strip of forest that wound along Spring River and up into the bluffs. This was the main reason we traveled there, the woods made for fantastic camping! While my grandfather would tend to the farm, check up on the crops, and maybe chase the neighbor's cows back across the fence, we'd pitch our tents on the bank of the river and spend a week swimming, hiking, and exploring."

"I was always excited for a hike into the backwoods. It always felt like an adventure back in time, from the rustic buildings near the edge to the depths of the forest that were so dense you almost needed a flashlight to see in the middle of the day. My sisters, cousins, and I would explore the woods for hours until we could barely walk back to

camp. Even in the depths of a muggy Missouri July, Spring River was still cold enough to take your breath away thanks to the springs that fed it. There was nothing more refreshing than jumping in after a hike up the bluffs. Then, we'd get a bite to eat and doze off on a quilt spread out in the shade."

"As the years went on, I grew up and moved out from my parents' house, and got a job and responsibilities of my own that made summertime go by faster than ever before. Yet, I still find the time to go back down to the farm and relive those precious childhood memories. Every time I return, it's as if nothing has changed since I was a kid. Sure, a tree or two might have fallen and the river shifted a bit, but I can still find the old barn, trails, and favorite fishing spots, and the river's just as chilly and refreshing as before. So, while time keeps slipping by, I still have a place to go that's just like summers past."

materials

QUILT SIZE
71" x 79"

BLOCK SIZE
16" finished

QUILT TOP
1 package 10" print squares
1 package 10" background squares

INNER BORDER
½ yard

OUTER BORDER
1¼ yards

BINDING
¾ yard

BACKING
5 yards - vertical seam(s)

SAMPLE QUILT
Blue Symphony by Kanvas Studios for Benartex

1 make half-square triangle units

Select 28 print and 28 background 10" squares. Draw a line from corner to corner twice on the diagonal on the reverse side of each background square. Layer a marked background square with a print square with right sides facing. Sew on both sides of each line using a ¼" seam allowance. Cut each set of sewn squares in half vertically and horizontally, then cut on the drawn lines. Square each half-square triangle unit to 4½". Open and press the seam allowance toward the dark fabric. Each set of sewn squares will yield 8 half-square triangles and a **total of 224** are needed for the quilt. **1A**

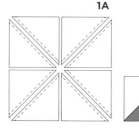

1A

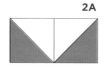

2A

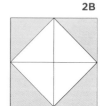

2B

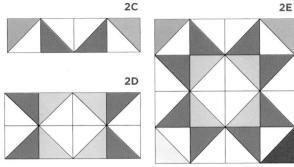

2C

2D

2E

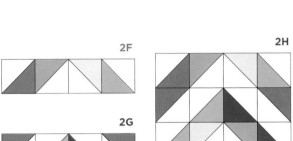

2F

2G

2H

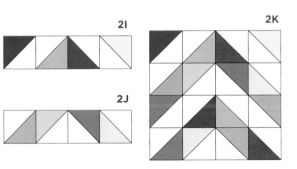

2I

2J

2K

2 block construction

Block A

Pick up 8 matching half-square triangle units for the star points. Add 4 other matching half-square triangle units for the center of the star. Add 4 more half-square triangle units for the corners of the block.

Sew 2 matching half-square triangle units together to make 1 star point unit. Make 4. **2A**

Pick up the 4 matching half-square triangle units you are using for the center of the block. Sew the 4 together in a 4-patch formation as shown. Set aside for the moment. **2B**

Sew a corner half-square triangle unit to either end of a star point unit. Make 2 rows like this. **2C**

Sew a star point unit to both sides of the center unit. **2D**

Sew the 3 rows together to complete 1 block. **Make 5. 2E**

Block Size: 16″ finished

Block B

Select 16 half-square triangle units. Sew 4 units together arranged as shown to make rows 1 and 3 of the block. **2F**

Sew 4 units together arranged as shown to make rows 2 and 4. **2G**

Sew the 4 rows together to complete Block B. **Make 2. 2H**

Block Size: 16″ finished

Block C

Select 16 half-square triangle units. Sew 4 units together arranged as shown to make rows 1 and 3 of the block. **2I**

Sew 4 units together arranged as shown to make rows 2 and 4. **2J**

Sew the 4 rows together to complete Block C. **Make 2. 2K**

Block Size: 16″ finished

3 arrange and sew

Lay out the quilt blocks in rows. Rows 1 and 3 begin and end with Block A. Block B is placed between Block A. Be aware of the direction Block B is placed.

The center row begins and ends with Block C. Block A is the center block. Again, be aware of the way Block C is oriented.

Before sewing all the rows together, you will need to make 2 sashing strips. Each strip is made by sewing 12 half-square triangle units together. Arrange the units as shown and sew them together. **3A**

Sew all the rows together, adding a sashing strip between rows 1 and 2 and between rows 2 and 3. See the diagram on page 85, if necessary.

4 inner border

Cut (6) 2½″ strips across the width of the background fabric. Sew the strips together end-to-end to make 1 long strip. Trim the borders from this strip.

3A

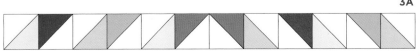

1 On the reverse side of a 10″ background square, draw a line from corner to corner twice on the diagonal. Layer a marked square with a print square with right sides facing. Sew on both sides of the drawn lines using a ¼″ seam allowance. Cut the sewn squares in half vertically and horizontally, then cut on the drawn lines.

2 Sew 2 matching half-square triangle units together to make each star point unit.

3 Pick up the 4 matching half-square triangle units being used for the center of the block and sew them together in a 4-patch formation.

4 Sew a half-square triangle unit to either side of a star point to make the top and bottom rows of the star block. Sew a star point to either side of the center unit to make the middle row. Sew the 3 rows together to complete 1 star block (Block A).

5 Select 16 half-square triangle units. Arrange as shown in 4 rows of 4. Sew the rows together to complete Block B.

6 To make Block C, select 16 half-square triangle units. Arrange as shown in 4 rows of 4. Sew the rows together to complete the block.

Sew a strip of 13 half-square triangle units together and add a 4½" background square to each end of the strip. Make 2 borders in this manner and sew 1 to the top of the quilt and 1 to the bottom. Refer to the diagram on the left and notice how the units are oriented. If necessary, adjust the length of the strip by either taking in a few seams or using a scant ¼" seam allowance in several places.

6 outer border

Cut (7) 6" strips across the width of the fabric. Sew the strips together end-to-end to make one long strip. Trim the borders from this strip.

Refer to Borders (pg. 102) in the Construction Basics to measure and cut the outer borders. The strips are approximately 68½" for the sides and approximately 71½" for the top and bottom.

7 quilt and bind

Layer the quilt with batting and backing and quilt. After the quilting is complete, square up the quilt and trim away all excess batting and backing. Add binding to complete the quilt. See Construction Basics (pg. 102) for binding instructions.

Refer to Borders (pg. 102) in the Construction Basics to measure and cut the inner borders. The strips are approximately 56½" for the sides and approximately 52½" for the top and bottom.

5 pieced border

Measure the quilt top through the center vertically in several places. Your measurement should be approximately 60½". Sew a strip of 15 half-square triangle units together to make the side border. Make 2 and sew 1 to either side of the quilt. Refer to the diagram above and notice how the units are oriented. If the strip doesn't come out perfectly to your measurement, use a scant ¼" seam allowance in several places if the border is too short. If it's too long, use a larger seam allowance in several places until the fit is correct.

Measure the quilt through the center horizontally in 2 or 3 places. It should measure approximately 60½" across. Pick up 1 of the remaining 10" background squares. Cut the square into (4) 4½" squares. Set aside for the moment.

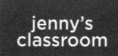
Building a Magazine Block by Block

When I saw the first issue of Block, I was stunned. It was just beautiful! It was so amazing to finally hold it in my hands. A lot has changed since that first issue, but Block remains a labor of love. We absolutely love what we do and we want to share how it all comes together. It's a pretty amazing process!

Block Magazine began with a big idea. We kept getting great feedback from our customers that they wanted patterns to go along with our videos, along with a subscription option, and they wished they could order the patterns right away and not have them run out and go away forever. That was a big one for us! New customers find us all the time and they want to read about who we are, get the patterns for the tutorials, and follow along with our story. So we started thinking. We wanted to make our very own pattern book filled with Missouri Star quilts and our original stories, and we did.

Each issue of Block starts with thoughtful planning months in advance. When I do a tutorial each Friday, it usually comes out in the next issue of Block. We take all our best ideas and put them into each beautiful, ad-free magazine, just for you! It's published every other month, with the addition of our yearly modern quilting magazine called ModBlock, which is sold separately from a Block subscription.

If you haven't checked it out yet, give it a try! It's honestly one of my favorite issues each year.

From concept to printed copy, Block comes together in about 4 months. Each issue begins with ten quilt designs from our weekly tutorials, paired with upcoming fabric collections. Together with my daughter, Natalie, we design quilts. Once we get the precut fabric and the yardage, I start mulling over ideas. I have a big file of ideas! I'll try a lot of different things. Sometimes I'll cut a block in half or snowball a corner. Because I don't design on a computer, I feel very free to add whatever design element I'd like. Everything I do is super simple. When I see a pattern I like, my brain figures out how to do it quicker or easier. It's so much fun to unravel the patterns behind old blocks and remake them in my own way.

Once Natalie and I settle on an idea, then we flesh it out and make it to be sure it's going to work. For every pattern, I have to sew at least one sample quilt myself because if I don't make it, I can't teach it in a tutorial. Once Natalie and I have complete quilt tops all stitched up, they are sent over to our sewists, Carol and Janice, who remake the quilts with new fabrics selected for each issue and send them off to the quilting and binding department, which includes about 20 skilled longarmers. The quilts have batting and backing added and are quilted up on big longarm quilting machines. The final step to creating the quilts is when the sewists carefully add on the binding.

Meanwhile, the pattern team, Edie, Denise, Jessica, and Tyler, takes each beautiful, handcrafted quilt top or project and breaks the design down into steps, figuring out precut fabric and yardage requirements, and noting when any tools or templates are needed. Then, they outline the sewing process, piece by piece, so you have a visual of how the block comes together. Finally, the finished quilt is shown in its entirety. But we're not through yet!

As the quilts are being made and before the photos are taken, our writers, Camille, David, Julie, and Nichole, are hard at work crafting heartfelt stories to accompany the quilts. Our copywriters get a list of article notes and ideas. They write the articles and send them back to me and Natalie for review and edits. Once they are approved, the articles are ready to be put into the magazine. The stories often start with my family and memorable moments from our lives, but we also collect stories from friends and quilters all over the world who share their unique perspectives. In ModBlock, each contributing designer writes their own article to accompany their original quilt design.

jenny's classroom

When the quilts are complete, the photography team comes in. Mike, Lauren, and Jennifer often spend weeks planning out destinations for their photoshoots, scouting locations and acquiring props to make each photo special. For an entire week, the ten quilts are photographed in picturesque places surrounding Missouri Star and beyond. We like to use family members, local friends, and employees as models. Our team does a great job of setting up photos that reflect the subject of the articles. We take styled shots, flat shots, photos of the materials used to make the quilt, and photos of the sewing process. After the photos are finished, they are sent off to our photo retoucher, Dustin, who makes sure they really shine.

As the stories and photographs are finished, the layout comes together. The creative director, Christine, orchestrates all the efforts of the contributing team members to make each beautiful issue come to life. She's present to help guide the photoshoot and then she works on the overall design of the magazine. When she's through, the pattern team, copywriters, designers and photography team all work together to proof the magazine several times once it's complete to ensure it's the best it can be!

Finally, Rob, our jack-of-all-trades and printing coordinator, schedules all the last-minute details. He'd ship each issue of Block out personally, but we have a wonderful warehouse crew who takes care of that! After the magazine is sent to print, all the other info is added to the website so Block is available to buy online as soon as it returns from the printer and lands in the warehouse. By the time Block arrives in your mailbox, it's been on a long journey and it's glad to finally be home.

FUN FACTS

- The first issue of Block was printed in 2014
- 39 issues of Block have been printed, including 5 issues of ModBlock
- Over 40 people work together to plan, create, and publish each issue of Block
- It takes about 4 months to create each complete issue of Block
- Block is printed locally in Missouri
- All the quilt designs, stories, and photography are original works of art
- Block doesn't require ad revenue, it relies on subscriptions from readers like you
- Over 60 original quilts and other fun projects are made each year for Block

jenny's classroom

berry
season

QUILT SIZE
48" x 48"

BLOCK SIZE
3" x 3½" finished

QUILT TOP
2 packages 5" print squares
2 packages 5" background squares
¼ yard matching background fabric

BORDER
¾ yard

BINDING
½ yard

BACKING
3¼ yards - horizontal seam(s)

OTHER
Missouri Star Small Simple Wedge
Template

SAMPLE QUILT
Cinnaberry by 3 Sisters for
Moda Fabrics

ONLINE TUTORIALS
msqc.co/blocksummer19

PATTERN
pg. 70

courtyard path

QUILT SIZE
79" x 95"

BLOCK SIZE
8" finished

QUILT TOP
1 package 10" print squares
1 package 10" background squares

INNER BORDER
¾ yard

OUTER BORDER
1¾ yards

BINDING
¾ yard

BACKING
8½ yards - vertical seam(s) - or 3 yards of
108" wide

OTHER SUPPLIES
Missouri Star Drunkard's Path Small Circle
Template Set

SAMPLE QUILT
Misty by Chong-a Hwang for Timeless
Treasures

ONLINE TUTORIALS
msqc.co/blocksummer19

PATTERN
pg. 14

easy
clamshell

QUILT SIZE
59" x 67"

BLOCK SIZE
4" finished

QUILT TOP
4 matching packages 5" print squares

BORDER
1¼ yards

BINDING
¾ yard

BACKING
3¾ yards - horizontal seam(s)

OTHER
Missouri Star Drunkard's Path Small Circle Template Set

SAMPLE QUILT
Regency Sussex by Christopher Wilson-Tate for Moda Fabrics

ONLINE TUTORIALS
msqc.co/blocksummer19

PATTERN
pg. 22

turnabout granny squares

QUILT SIZE
65" x 78"

BLOCK SIZE
11" finished

QUILT TOP
1 roll 2½" print strips
1 roll 2½" background strips -
  includes inner border

OUTER BORDER
1¼ yards

BINDING
¾ yard

BACKING
4¾ yards - vertical seam(s)

SAMPLE QUILT
Sweet Stems by Sue Daley Designs
for Riley Blake Designs

ONLINE TUTORIALS
msqc.co/blocksummer19

PATTERN
pg. 38

leafy
tree tops

TABLE RUNNER SIZE
24" x 54"

BLOCK SIZE
6" finished

TABLE RUNNER TOP
1 package of 5" print squares
¾ yard background fabric
   -includes inner border

OUTER BORDER
½ yard

BINDING
½ yard

BACKING
1¾ yards - horizontal seam(s)

SAMPLE QUILT
Artisan Batiks Round and Around
by Lunn Studios for Robert Kaufman

ONLINE TUTORIALS
msqc.co/blocksummer19

PATTERN
pg. 46

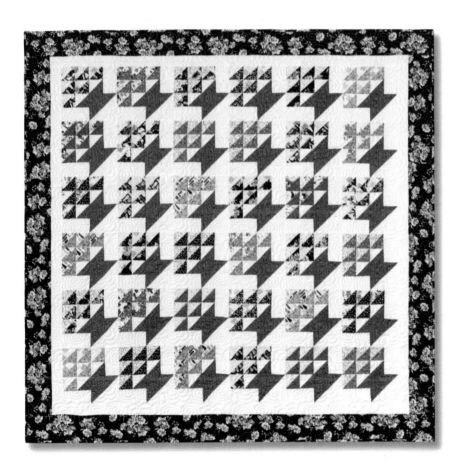

may day baskets

QUILT SIZE
73" x 73"

BLOCK SIZE
10" finished

QUILT TOP
1 roll 2½" print strips
2½ yards background fabric
  -includes inner border
1 yard complementary print fabric

OUTER BORDER
1¼ yards

BINDING
¾ yard

BACKING
4½ yards - vertical seam(s)

OTHER
Clearly Perfect Slotted Trimmers

SAMPLE QUILT
Field Day by Kelly Ventura for
Windham Fabrics

ONLINE TUTORIALS
msqc.co/blocksummer19

PATTERN
pg. 54

night
sky

QUILT SIZE
71" x 79"

BLOCK SIZE
16" finished

QUILT TOP
1 package 10" print squares
1 package 10" background squares

INNER BORDER
½ yard

OUTER BORDER
1¼ yards

BINDING
¾ yard

BACKING
5 yards - vertical seam(s)

SAMPLE QUILT
Blue Symphony by Kanvas Studios
for Benartex

ONLINE TUTORIALS
msqc.co/blocksummer19

PATTERN
pg. 78

rickrack

QUILT SIZE
75" x 75"

BLOCK SIZE
10" finished

QUILT TOP
1 roll 2½" print strips
1 roll 2½" background strips

INNER BORDER
¼ yard

OUTER BORDER
1¼ yards

BINDING
¾ yard

BACKING
4¾ yards - vertical seam(s)

SAMPLE QUILT
Graphic Jewels Batiks by Kathy
Engle for Island Batiks

ONLINE TUTORIALS
msqc.co/blocksummer19

PATTERN
pg. 62

tilted nine-patch

QUILT SIZE
71" x 71"

BLOCK SIZE
10" finished

QUILT TOP
1 roll 2½" print strips
1 roll 2½" background strips

BORDER
1¼ yards

BINDING
¾ yard

BACKING
4½ yards - vertical seam(s)

SAMPLE QUILT
Imperial Collection 15 by Studio RK
for Robert Kaufman

ONLINE TUTORIALS
msqc.co/blocksummer19

PATTERN
pg. 30

vintage blossom

QUILT SIZE
70" x 84"

BLOCK SIZE
12" finished

QUILT TOP
4 packages 5" print squares
1 roll 2½" background strips
  -includes inner border

OUTER BORDER
1½ yards

BINDING
¾ yard

BACKING
5¼ yards - vertical seam(s)

OTHER
Missouri Star Small Half-Hexagon
Template

SAMPLE QUILT
Red and Blue... and Roses Too! by
Faye Burgos for Marcus Fabrics

ONLINE TUTORIALS
msqc.co/blocksummer19

PATTERN
pg.6

construction basics

general quilting

- All seams are ¼" unless directions specify differently.
- Precuts are not prewashed; so do not prewash other fabrics in the project.
- Remove all selvages.

press seams

- Set the temperature of the iron on the cotton setting.
- Set the seam by pressing it just as it was sewn, right sides together.
- Place the darker fabric on top, lift, and press back.
- Press seam allowances toward the borders unless directed otherwise.

borders

- Always measure the quilt top in 3 different places vertically before cutting side borders.
- Start measuring about 4" in from the top and bottom.
- Take the average of those 3 measurements.
- Cut 2 border strips to that size. Piece strips together if needed.
- Attach one to either side of the quilt. Position the border fabric on top as you sew to prevent waviness and to keep the quilt straight.
- Repeat this process for the top and bottom borders, measuring the width 3 times. Include the newly attached side borders in your measurements.

backing

- Measure the quilt top vertically and horizontally. Add 8" to both measurements to make sure you have an extra 4" all the way around to make allowance for the fabric that is taken up in the quilting process as well as having adequate fabric for the quilting frame.
- Trim off all selvages and use a ½" seam allowance when piecing the backing. Sew the pieces together along the longest edge. Press the seam allowance open to decrease bulk.
- Use horizontal seams for smaller quilts (under 60" wide), vertical seams for larger quilts.
- Don't hesitate to cut a length of fabric in half along the fold line if it means saving fabric and makes the quilt easier to handle.
- Choose a backing layout that best suits your quilt. Note: large quilts might require 3 lengths.

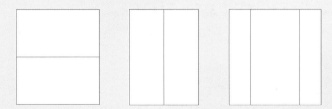

binding

find a video tutorial at: www.msqc.co/006

- Use 2½" strips for binding.
- Sew strips together end-to-end into one long strip using diagonal seams, a.k.a. plus sign method (next). Press seams open.
- Fold in half lengthwise with wrong sides together and press.
- The entire length should equal the outside dimension of the quilt plus 15" - 20".

plus sign method

find a video tutorial at: www.msqc.co/001

- Lay one strip across the other
  as if to make a plus sign right sides together.
- Sew from top inside to bottom outside corners crossing the
  intersections of fabric as you sew. Trim the excess fabric ¼"
  away from the sewn seam.
- Press seam(s) open.

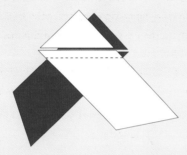

attach binding

- Match raw edges of the folded binding to one edge of the
  top of the quilt.
- Leave a 10" tail at the beginning.
- Use a ¼" seam allowance.
- Start sewing in the middle of a long straight side.

miter corners

- Stop sewing ¼" before the corner.
- Move the quilt out from under the presser foot.
- Flip the binding up at a 90° angle to the edge just sewn.
- Fold the binding down along the next side to be sewn,
  aligning raw edges.
- The fold will lie along the edge just completed.
- Begin sewing on the fold.

close binding

- Stop sewing when you have 12" left to reach the start.
- Where the binding tails come together, trim excess
  leaving only 2½" of overlap.
- Pin or clip the quilt together at the two points where
  the binding starts and stops to take the pressure off of
  the binding tails.
- Use the plus sign method to sew the two binding ends
  together, except this time, match the edges. Using a
  pencil, mark your sewing line and stitch.
- Trim off excess; press the seam open.
- Fold in half with wrong sides together and align all raw
  edges to the quilt top.
- Sew this last binding section to the quilt. Press.
- Turn the folded edge of the binding around to the back
  of the quilt and tack in place with an invisible stitch or
  machine stitch.

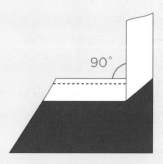

90°

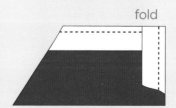

fold